THE CRITICS DEBATE

General Editor: Michael Scott

THE METAPHYSICAL POETS

Donald Mackenzie

MACMILLAN

To my mother and to the memory of my father

First published 1990

PR
545
m4
m43
1990

Published by
MACMILLAN EDUCATION LTD
Houndmills, Basingstoke, Hampshire RG21 2XS
and London
Companies and representatives throughout the world

Printed in Hong Kong

British Library Cataloguing in Publication Data
Mackenzie, Donald
The metaphysical poets.—(The critics debate).
1. Metaphysical poetry in English, 1558–1702 — Critical
studies
I. Title II. Series
821'.3'09
ISBN 0–333–44058–7
ISBN 0–333–44059–5 pbk

Contents

General Editor's Preface

OVER THE last few years the practice of literary criticism has become hotly debated. Methods developed earlier in the century and before have been attacked and the word 'crisis' has been drawn upon to describe the present condition of English Studies. That such a debate is taking place is a sign of the subject discipline's health. Some would hold that the situation necessitates a radical alternative approach which naturally implies a 'crisis situation'. Others would respond that to employ such terms is to precipitate or construct a false position. The debate continues but it is not the first. 'New Criticism' acquired its title because it attempted something fresh, calling into question certain practices of the past. Yet the practices it attacked were not entirely lost or negated by the new critics. One factor becomes clear: English Studies is a pluralistic discipline.

What are students coming to advanced work in English for the first time to make of all this debate and controversy? They are in danger of being overwhelmed by the cross-currents of critical approaches as they take up their study of literature. The purpose of this series is to help delineate various critical approaches to specific literary texts. Its authors are from a variety of critical schools and have approached their task in a flexible manner. Their aim is to help the reader come to terms with the variety of criticism and to introduce him or her to further reading on the subject and to a fuller evaluation of a particular text by illustrating the way it has been approached in a number of contexts. In the first part of the book a critical survey is given of some of the major ways the text has been appraised. This is done sometimes in a thematic manner, sometimes according to various 'schools' or 'approaches'. In the second part the authors provide their own appraisals of the tex from their stated critical standpoint, allowing the reader th knowledge of their own particular approaches from whic their views may in turn be evaluated. The series therei hopes to introduce and to elucidate criticism of author and texts being studied and to encourage participation a the critics debate.

Michael Scot

Note on Texts

Carew's Elegy on Donne is quoted from *The Cavalier Poets*, ed. T. Clayton. Donne, Vaughan and Marvell are quoted from the respective Penguin editions (see References); Crashaw is quoted from the *Complete Poetry*, ed. G. Williams and Herbert from the *Works*, ed. F. E. Hutchinson.

The Penguin editions modernise spelling: those of Herbert and Crashaw do not. Readers should note that this may have the effect of making the latter, and especially Crashaw, seem more exotic than, in their seventeenth–century context, they are.

Acknowledgements

The author and publishers wish to thank the following for permission to use copyright material:

Chatto & Windus on behalf of Lady Empson with Harcourt Brace Jovanovich, Inc. for 'Missing Dates' from *Collected Poems* by William Empson. Copyright © 1949, renewed 1977 by William Empson;
Doubleday & Co. for an extract from 'Matthew, 22, Neither durst any man from that Day aske him any more Questions' in *The Complete Poems of Richard Crashaw* ed. G. W. Williams. Copyright © 1970 by Doubleday & Co. on intro., notes and compilation.

Every effort has been made to trace all the copyright holders, but if any have been inadvertently overlooked the publishers will be pleased to make the necessary arrangement at the first opportunity.

Introduction

THE SUBJECT of this book – the Metaphysical poets – has dictated a plan somewhat different from that of most studies in the series. I have taken Metaphysical simply as a long-settled label for some English poets in the first half of the seventeenth century without raising any question about whether their activity as poets has something in common with the branch of philosophical enquiry known as metaphysics. The Metaphysical poets are simply the poets commonly classed as such and I have concentrated on five – Donne, Herbert, Crashaw, Vaughan and Marvell – with side glances at other figures. These include not only minor Metaphysicals like Cleveland and Cowley but Carew and Lovelace from the 'Cavalier' group of lyric poets in the 1630s and 1640s. As a group the latter are sometimes linked to the dominant figure of Jonson earlier in the century but the two I have picked out belong at least as much with the Metaphysicals. Carew could be claimed as Donne's most direct disciple and Lovelace, I shall argue, offers the most immediate context for the lyrics of Marvell.

Not only does this study consider five poets, as against a single text or two texts, but its poets have received intensive critical attention from the late 1920s on. The Survey accordingly makes no attempt at completeness and the Appraisal is strictly rationed in detailed comment on their work. In the space available it would have been impossible to summarise all the criticism of Metaphysical poetry that is of interest or value. When discussing critics of the individual poets I have therefore begun in each case with studies, whether book or essay, which will give the reader of Donne or Marvell or whoever an overall view of their work and raise some of the main issues which their critics have debated. I have followed this with suggestions (highly selective) for reading in more specialised areas. The student who wishes to pursue these further will want to consult more detailed bibliographies.

In addition to criticism of the individual poets I have listed some background or context studies, together with literary histories and editions because all of these can shape the way we read texts and I take criticism to be, fundamentally, the conscious formulation of our reading.

I have sought to balance out this selective account by a more detailed analysis of the three seminal responses to Metaphysical poetry, by Johnson, Coleridge and Eliot. I have analysed these at some length because they articulate the fundamental issues Metaphysical poetry raises and, in so doing, bring out the differences and continuity in response to it across a century and a half.

The differences are more immediately striking than the continuities. The three accounts differ most obviously in the strategies through which they articulate their responses to Metaphysical poetry. By strategies I mean the kind of analysis they practise, the comparisons they make, in defining this poetry and in judging its value. To elucidate these strategies brings out the differences in the concepts deployed and the assumptions underlying their reading of it. Such differences, in turn, reach back into the differing contexts of culture and history out of which as critics Johnson and the others write. And to become aware of such differences can be illuminating.

It is also illuminating, however, to register the continuity between those accounts, a continuity thrown up by the central question Metaphysical poetry presses on its readers. We make preliminary gestures towards defining this question when we speak of Metaphysical poetry as bizarre, striking, extravagant, quaint or grotesque. This first part of the Survey considers the response of those critics to this question; I come back to it at various points in the Appraisal and finally take it up in the Conclusion.

The problem in the Appraisal is that limits of space forbid extended quotation and analysis. At the same time I do not want to offer general accounts that are not pegged to individual poems. I have met this problem in two ways: first, by eliciting what seem to me key patterns in the work of an individual poet – Herbert's exploring of his own vocation, for instance, or the role of oxymoron in Crashaw; secondly, by naming poems and suggesting connections even when I do not analyse so that the reader can test my comments against specific poems. (This means that the Appraisal very much needs to be read after or alongside a reading of the poems in question; but that is as it should be.)

Between the survey of criticism and the accounts of individual poets I have given a statement of my own approach, through the analysis of style, and an overview of the development of the distinctive Metaphysical style from Donne to Marvell. Development should be stressed. My analysis of style is both formalist and historical and the second partly because it is the first. It is formalist in that it begins from the forms the Metaphysicals use. I take forms in the widest sense possible: metrical forms, syntactic forms, the forms dictated by conventions of stance and genre and diction. Any extended analysis of such forms is, and must be, historical. One can try to abstract the forms that poets use and consider them as unchanging templates or frames; but the study of such abstracted forms will yield at best limited insights and if applied over any extended stretch of literature becomes absurd. It becomes absurd because poetic forms exist not in some timeless realm but only as they are used by poets; and to be used means to be modified, extended, renewed; to be found cramping or obsolete or finally unusable, and so to be discarded. The study of forms is the study of their history; the study of a poetic style becomes, to borrow the title of Barbara Everett's luminous collection of essays, a study of *Poets in their Time*.

As that title underlines, poets write in specific times and places and these contexts help to mould the meanings they create. Our understanding of any utterance comes from the interplay between the known meaning of its individual items and the context in which they occur. This holds at every level from monosyllabic cry or command up through individual sentences to such enormously complex 'utterances' as *Hamlet* or *Paradise Lost*. Any utterance, be it a single sentence or an epic, creates a context for the items that compose it. But it needs a larger context to be understood fully, sometimes to be understood at all. Hence the need with poetry from the past for the *recovery* – the *proper* recovery – of contexts which may be unknown or alien. This is the second sense in which the approach of this study is historical.

I stress *proper* because the number of possible contexts is various and indefinite and one cannot specify in advance which contexts will illuminate a text. To define an apt context and bring it to bear requires tact. It requires curiosity and a disciplined attention to the text which is the commanding centre from which enquiry should begin.

In Part Two I have glanced at a variety of contexts for the Metaphysical poets: at the literature of the 1590s as a context for the early Donne; at the programme for a sacred poetry and at some New Testament metaphors as contexts for Herbert; at the prolonged upheavals of mid-century politics as contexts for Vaughan and Marvell – but also at some permanent tensions in Christianity as a context for the former and at some Cavalier lyrics as a context for the latter. (The crossing of different *kinds* of context is deliberate.) I have perhaps concentrated on the contexts offered by other texts and writers, whether as models or as masters or as analogues or merely in passing comparisons. If this seems to leave the Appraisal studded with unelaborated names and references readers may take comfort from C.S. Lewis's account of his first encounter with Arnold's *Sohrab and Rustum* at his Ulster public school: 'I loved the poem' he says 'at first sight and have loved it ever since.'

> And here observe how literature actually works. Parrot critics say that *Sohrab* is a poem for classicists, to be enjoyed only by those who recognize the Homeric echoes. But ... for me the relation between Arnold and Homer worked the other way; when I came, years later, to read the *Iliad* I liked it partly because it was for me reminiscent of *Sohrab*. Plainly, it does not matter at what point you break into the system of European poetry. Only keep your ears open and your mouth shut and everything will lead you to everything else in the end.

I am indebted to various friends and colleagues: to Stuart Gillespie for discussion of seventeenth-century literary history and for letting me see an unpublished paper on Cowley; to Louise Henderson for conversations on Donne; to David Newell and Nancy Scerbo for comments on Herbert; and especially to Robert Cummings and Sandra Kemp who read and criticised sections of the book in draft. My largest debts are indicated in the dedication.

Part One:
Survey

A Critick, one *ingeniosus in alienis*, overwitty in other men's business.

[Donne]

We judge a work of art by its effect on our sincere and vital emotion, and nothing else. All the critical twiddle-twaddle about style and form, all this pseudo-scientific classifying and analysing of books in an imitation-botanical fashion is mere impertinence and mostly dull jargon.

[Lawrence]

Criticism should be partisan, passionate, political, that is to say, shaped by a point of view that excludes but one that opens up the widest horizons.

[Baudelaire]

The seminal critics: Johnson, Coleridge, Eliot

The Metaphysicals are one of the Cinderellas – perhaps the most striking – of English poetry. A major, if not the dominant, body of poets in their own period they are eclipsed (as Spenser, Shakespeare and Milton are not) in the changes of poetic style and of culture that take place in the decades after 1660, to be reclaimed as a major force in the wake of Eliot's revolutionary–into–classic essays of the 1920s. So at least the myth would run; the history, as always, is less incisive, more varied.

In some cases the eclipse has proved permanent. Cowley, acclaimed in his day as one of the greatest English poets, is now read only by specialists and the occasional random general reader who is likely to find his lyrics in the Metaphysical style imitative and limp – Donne poems rewritten on blotting paper – and his Pindaric Odes a creaky extravagance. Elsewhere he can still be, for such a reader, quietly rewarding: in his versions of the drinking songs attributed to the Greek lyric poet Anacreon; in elegy; in the translations scattered through his essays. For the specialist his value can be documentary or historical: Trotter [1979] argues that his poetry manifests major shifts in modes of thinking during the seventeenth century. Through them both his poetry sustains an attenuated life. But it does not command our imagination as the poetry of Donne, Herbert, Marvell still can. We can expand this judgment to say that Cowley – certainly as a Metaphysical poet – has not *counted*, as they have, in the subsequent history of literature.

And yet that is not quite the end of the matter. Gillespie [1988] judges Cowley's Anacreontics 'the most inward and appealing' recreations in English of the originals [p.68]. And to read him in historical context need not imply that his interest is *only* historical, the poems merely documents. Trotter argues that Cowley can make successful poems out of the difficulties created for him by his historical situation [e.g. 1979, pp.51–5 or 79–82] and asserts the value of the Pindaric Odes as responding to the radical and unsettling theory of knowledge propounded by Hobbes [pp.109f].

What all this brings out is the complexity of literary history, the number of factors that can come into play to determine how a poet continues to be read, whether he continues to live. Tomlinson, for instance, prizes Cowley's translations [1983, pp.81-4] in the context of a larger argument about the role translation can play in literature. And what is true of Cowley holds no less for the greater Metaphysicals. Herbert, though eclipsed as a poet from the late seventeenth to the early nineteenth century, continues to be mediated through devotional contexts. Poems of his are included in a Puritan hymn book of 1697 and rewritten for a similar purpose by Wesley. His disciple Vaughan enjoys a largely, though not entirely, misconceived nineteenth-century reputation as a kind of proto-Wordsworth. Donne, the founding genius of Metaphysical poetry, though a marginal figure in the eighteenth century sustains a flickering interest that strengthens among the Romantics and grows quietly in the century that follows up to Grierson's major scholarly edition of 1912. (Tillotson in Roberts [1975, pp.20–33]; Duncan [1953].) The same editor's 1921 anthology, *Metaphysical Poetry from Donne to Butler*, provides a pendant to his Donne with an introduction that is still a rewarding survey of the field. Reviewing it in *The Times Literary Supplement* Eliot wrote the essay on 'The Metaphysical Poets' which, along with his 'Andrew

Marvell', ranks with Johnson's critique in the *Life of Cowley* and the comments strewn by Coleridge in various places as one of the three classic accounts of those writers.

For if their history makes the Metaphysicals a Cinderella they have at least been happy in their critics. The three I have taken as seminal write in different forms and out of very different contexts. Johnson mounts his critique in the course of a biographical essay; Coleridge's notes are mostly written in the margins of his own or friends' copies of the Metaphysicals or garnered in corners of that ramshackle work of genius his *Biographia Literaria*; while Eliot turns a journal review into a sketch history of three centuries of English poetry astonishing in its assurance and speed.

What make all three classic are, first, their blending of finality with a permanent power to suggest or provoke. They present (Johnson and Eliot especially) formulations that strike home as definitive: what many readers have dimly felt is here crystallised. At the same time those formulations seem to ask for expansion or challenge (though too often receiving only a ritual repetition). They are classic, secondly, in the range and centrality of the issues they imply, in their unforced involvement of questions of literature with questions of history, religion, society. They are classic, finally, in being rooted so emphatically in specific contexts of time and culture with the limitations these impose but also with the power they can give to order and to probe.

The limitations imposed by time and culture we are now sufficiently removed from all three of them to see clearly. Johnson writes at the end of the Augustan period in English literature and culture which reaches from the Restoration into the later eighteenth century. It is a culture confident in its own standards and in their universal validity but also capable of nourishing complex relations with some decidedly different literature from earlier periods. Johnson is one of the last major voices of this culture – indeed a belated one by the time the *Lives of the Poets* were being written in the late 1770s – and his critique draws some of its power from the trenchant genius with which he marshalls and intensifies some of the Augustan assumptions. Eliot's context (or one of them) is given by his own work as a major innovating poet, his sense of what needs to be called into play for poetry now. Coleridge seems, of the three, the least directed by a context, the most purely an acute general reader. But even his

praise of the neutral style of some Metaphysical poetry takes its
rise from his arguments with Wordsworth's theories on poetic
diction, and his discussions of Wit and Fancy move towards
the definition of Imagination which is one of his central
preoccupations as a critic. In all of them the contexts that
limit their accounts of Metaphysical poetry also empower their
engagement with the problems it raises, an engagement that in
the end carries their discussions beyond those original contexts.
The questions they put to Metaphysical poetry are still questions
for us; the answers they have given may prompt our questions
in turn.

Johnson

All three of the seminal accounts are linked, as the Introduction has suggested, by a sense of Metaphysical poetry
as problematic and problematic because central to it is an
activity of mind and imagination that has been classified since
the seventeenth century as *wit*. And wit is not only problematic
in its workings but curiously difficult to define. It is interesting
to note how Johnson, who generalises more abstractly than either
of the other two, nonetheless (like Cowley in his 'Ode: Of Wit'
before him and like Eliot after) advances towards a definition of
it by way of negatives.

> If Wit be well described by Pope, as being 'that which has
> been often thought but was never before so well expressed,'
> they certainly never attained, nor ever sought it, for they endeav-
> oured to be singular in their thoughts, and were careless in their
> diction . . .If by a more noble and adequate conception that be
> considered as wit which is at once natural and new, that which,
> though not obvious, is, upon its first production, acknowledged
> to be just; if it be that which he that never found it wonders
> how he missed; to wit of this kind the metaphysical poets
> have seldom risen. Their thoughts are often new, but seldom
> natural; they are not obvious, but neither are they just; and
> the reader, far from wondering that he missed them, wonders
> more frequently by what perverseness of industry they were
> ever found.
> But Wit, abstracted from its effects upon the hearer, may be

more rigorously and philosophically considered as . . .a combination of dissimilar images, or discovery of occult resemblances in things apparently unlike. Of wit, thus defined, they have more than enough. The most heterogenous ideas are yoked by violence together; nature and art are ransacked for illustrations, comparisons, and allusions; their learning instructs and their subtlety surprises; but the reader commonly thinks his improvement dearly bought, and, though he sometimes admires, is seldom pleased. [1905, pp.19–20]

This passage carries several key assumptions of Johnson's criticism. First, there is a normative order in the world and in human experience, an order evoked by the interrelated terms 'natural' and 'just'. Metaphysical poetry with its violent yoking of heterogeneous ideas violates this order and produces a poetry striking but strained. Secondly, this appeal to the normative does not reduce literature to merely restating with elegance or force what is obvious or already known. Wit as defined by Pope falls, if anything, further short of Johnson's ideal than does the wit of the Metaphysicals. The products of that wit which he ranks highest are 'at once natural and new'. Thirdly, the final appeal is to the effect on the audience: 'Wit, *abstracted from its effects upon the hearer*, may be more rigorously and philosophically considered as . . .' But such abstraction is momentary and the final judgement decisive: 'the reader . . .though he sometimes admires, is seldom pleased'.

The appeal to the reader can combine the psychological (this is how literature affects us) with the moral (this is how literature ought to affect us) as the next paragraph, on the failure of the Metaphysicals (in Johnson's view) to move the emotions, makes clear:

As they were wholly employed on something unexpected and surprising, they had no regard to that uniformity of sentiment which enables us to conceive and excite the pains and the pleasure of other minds: they never inquired what on any occasion they should have said or done, but wrote rather as beholders than partakers of human nature.

We might gloss this by saying that for Johnson there is a community of feeling between human beings, a community created by shared experience. It is this community which enables us to conceive the pains and pleasures that other minds feel and it is only by conceiving them, of course, that writers can evoke them. The Metaphysicals, by refusing to respect this community, limit their own poetry: 'their courtship was void of fondness, and their lamentation of sorrow'. And in a final sentence Johnson nails this down in a judgement on their desire to surprise and impress: 'their wish was only to say what they hoped had been never said before'. The same desire which warps Metaphysical poetry intellectually cripples it in the evoking of emotion.

What we may well find alien in Johnson, while acknowledging its power, is the assurance with which he deploys his general concepts of human nature and the consequences he draws from them for poetry. We may consider the whole concept of an unchanging human nature problematic or questionable or untrue; even if we do not we may hold that concepts of human nature need to be more fluid and plural than Johnson would allow. We may place a higher value on individuality than he does, even on individuality as it spirals into the wilful or the idiosyncratic. Partly in consequence of this we may be willing to allow, or give a high place to, the pleasure that can be given by the extravagance which for him is the central defect of Metaphysical poetry.

Viewing Johnson's account as a whole we are struck by its *integration*. It begins from the abstract definitions of wit, proceeds to amplify these and in amplifying draws them tight in firm but nuanced judgements. The key concepts it deploys are highly general and it deploys them with a massive assurance. It is the interlocking of those concepts that gives the critique its integrated power – to reject or refute it one would have to call the concepts themselves or their relevance to Metaphysical poetry into question. This is, to some extent, the thrust of Coleridge's notes on Donne with their praise of the latter's extravagance. Or one might accept the validity of Johnson's terms, as, to some extent, Eliot does, but argue that the best of Metaphysical poetry either falls outside or transcends them. What either approach implicitly acknowledges is the force of Johnson's critique. He has formulated the central question that must be put to Metaphysical poetry: whether its distinctive style does not carry certain inherent limitations; or, rather, whether its inherent limitations do not disable it for some central activities of poetry. Metaphysical poetry may be able to transcend those limitations; if it is to meet Johnson's critique it *must*.

Coleridge

Coleridge's criticism of the Metaphysicals could hardly differ more in its procedure from Johnson's. It is largely occasional, headlong, metaphorical where Johnson defines and judges. It annotates individual poems where he brings the massed weight of his general terms to bear. But Coleridge's marginal notes, in their turn, swirl out into generalisations that are among the most illuminating we have. In one place (not among the Donne marginalia) he defines wit as consisting 'in presenting thoughts or images in an unusual connection with each other, for the purpose of exciting pleasure by the surprise' [Brinkley,1955, p.615]. This is close to Johnson's definition but neutral in tone – so neutral it needs the filling-out he gives it elsewhere:

> Wonder-exciting vigour, intenseness and peculiarity of thought, using at will the almost boundless stores of a capacious memory, and exercised on subjects where we have no right to expect it – this is the wit of Donne! [Brinkley, pp.526–7]

In another passage he relates this copiousness and energy to the masterfulness he sees at the heart of Donne's poetry:

> the will-worship, in squandering golden hecatombs on a Fetisch, on the first stick or straw met with at rising – this pride in doing what he likes with his own, fearless of an immense surplus to pay all lawful debts to self-subsisting themes . . . – this is Donne! [Brinkley, p.523]

Accounts of Donne from the beginning have stressed his masterfulness. What Coleridge illuminatingly does is to see his extravagance not as bewildering, still less perverse, but as an expression of such masterfulness. He also suggests the key element of *play* in this poetry – the space that its masterfulness creates to disport itself in; and in the next sentence claims that this strenuous, arrogant freedom of play penetrates Donne's most serious concerns: 'he was an orthodox Christian only because he could have been an infidel *more* easily; and, therefore, willed to be a Christian'.

That account of Donne should be balanced against the praise in *Biographia Literaria* [c.xix] of a middle or neutral style 'where the scholar and the poet supplies the material, but the perfect well-bred gentleman, the expressions and the arrangement', a style of which Herbert is saluted as an 'exquisite master'. Coleridge widens this into the claim that 'the characteristic fault of our elder poets' is their 'conveying the most fantastic thoughts in the most correct and natural language'. Fantastic here belongs with the family of adjectives – grotesque, extravagant, bizarre – recurrently used to characterise Metaphysical poetry and each carrying its distinctive nuance of judgement. 'Fantastic', I suggest, has the effect of making what it characterises more remote than, say, 'grotesque' or 'extravagant'. Metaphysical poetry under this heading seems lighter, less outrageous, to be taken less seriously. An earlier passage of the *Biographia* develops this implication by endeavouring to erect a distinction between Fancy and Imagination which leads into the famous formulation [c.xiv] of the Imagination as the power which 'reveals itself in the balance or reconcilement of opposite and discordant qualities'.

Eliot

Eliot weaves that passage, as also Johnson's critique, into his own account with the rapidity which is so striking a feature of 'The Metaphysical Poets' and 'Andrew Marvell'. In 'The Metaphysical Poets' he isolates the phrase we have seen to be the pivot of Johnson's critique ('the most heterogeneous ideas are yoked by force together'), observes that 'a degree of heterogeneity of material compelled into unity by the operation of the poet's mind is omnipresent in poetry' [1951, p.283] and reaches through a skilfully spaced series of quotations, one of them from Johnson himself, and a couple of remarks in passing on structure and music in Metaphysical poetry, to his key problematic formulations on the 'direct sensuous apprehension of thought' [p.286] in Chapman and Donne. In the Marvell essay he tacitly rebuts Coleridge's distinction between Imagination and Fancy, quoting the famous *Biographia Literaria* passage on the former and leaving it to interact in the reader's mind with the quotations from Marvell that follow [p.298]. In both essays he is mapping, like Johnson and unlike Coleridge, a literary history, but a history much more extended and mapped in terms more sweeping than Johnson employs. And he does so under the urge of a need which has no

equivalent in Johnson, the need to define the history in which
he finds himself in ways that will open that history to the poetry
that needs to be written now. Other major innovators in English
poetry have done this – Wordsworth very notably in the Preface
to the *Lyrical Ballads*, to a lesser degree Dryden. But no one has
deployed so elaborate a history in so brief a compass.

The brevity is secured partly through his myth of the
dissociation of sensibility. We shall have to come back to this
phrase and to why it is to be judged a myth that illuminates
much less than it misleads. What we may note for the moment
is the panache with which Eliot deploys it:

> In the seventeenth century a dissociation of sensibility set in
> from which we have never recovered . . . .The language went
> on and in some respects improved . . . .But while the language
> became more refined, the feeling became more crude . . . .in
> one or two passages of Shelley's *Triumph of Life*, in the second
> *Hyperion*, there are traces of a struggle towards unification of
> sensibility. But Keats and Shelley died, and Tennyson and
> Browning ruminated. [p.298]

The assured brevity of this exposition – 'too brief, perhaps,'
says Eliot in a deadpan parenthesis, 'to carry conviction' – is
about equally exhilarating and implausible. Yet it only carries
to an extreme features that characterise the procedure of both
essays: a habit of darting and weaving reference across wide
areas of literature and a style that cultivates the elliptical to
secure effects at once understated and magisterial.

If darting, however, Eliot's procedure at its best is dartingly
specific. (One might contrast it both with the exuberance of
Coleridge and Johnson's advance through generalities.) If, like
Johnson and Cowley, he advances to a definition of wit through
negatives both the negatives and the final formulation are nailed
down in specific and ranging examples.

> The wit of the Caroline poets is not the wit of Shakespeare,
> and it is not the wit of Dryden, the great master of contempt, or
> of Pope, the great master of hatred, or of Swift, the great master
> of disgust. What is meant is some quality which is common to
> the songs in *Comus* and Cowley's Anacreontics and Marvell's
> Horatian Ode. It is more than a technical accomplishment, or

the vocabulary and syntax of an epoch; it is, what we have designated tentatively as wit, a tough reasonableness beneath the slight lyric grace. [p.293]

A single turn-of-the-wrist movement can open those specificities into topics which will engage Eliot later, whether as social critic ('the unknown quality of which we speak is probably a literary rather than a personal quality; or, more truly . . .it is a quality of a civilization, of a traditional habit of life' [p.292]) or as religious poet ('this wisdom, cynical, perhaps, but untired (in Shakespeare a terrifying clairvoyance), leads toward, and is only completed by, the religious comprehension' [p.297]). And the final drive of both essays is to mould generalisation towards prescription for poetry now. The review of Grierson's anthology concludes that the Metaphysicals 'are in the direct current of English poetry, and . . .their faults should be reprimanded by this standard rather than coddled by antiquarian affection' [p.290]; 'Andrew Marvell' concludes that 'this modest and certainly impersonal virtue – whether we call it wit or reason, or even urbanity . . .is something precious and needed and apparently extinct' [p.304].

Of the three seminal accounts of Metaphysical poetry Eliot's is the most ambitious and vulnerable. It is both of these because it is the most thoroughly historical. Its pervasively historical mode emerges in various ways: in its handling (so different from Johnson's) of key terms; in the network of connections it establishes between the Metaphysicals and their age; in its myth of the dissociation of sensibility.

Both essays link the Metaphysicals with, if they do not assimilate them to, the Jacobean dramatists and to those nineteenth-century French poets, from Gautier to Laforgue, who were crucial to Eliot in the genesis of his own poetry up to *The Waste Land*. To note that the judgements of Eliot the critic interact in this way with the interests of Eliot the innovating poet does not necessarily invalidate the former. The question to be asked, as always, is: how far do they illuminate the texts we are reading? My own answer would be that 'The Metaphysical Poets' suggests a Donne closer to Webster than Donne really is, picking out the line 'A bracelet of bright hair about the bone' which is striking but not characteristic (the poem 'Whispers of Immortality' in Eliot's 1920 volume assimilates them more flamboyantly); and that, on the other hand, to claim that Marvell's *Horatian Ode* 'has that same quality of wit that was diffused over the whole Elizabethan product and concentrated in the work of Jonson' [p.301] is to generalise suggestively about an entire culture through a single poem. The potent historical myth of the dissociation of sensibility is another matter.

Dissociation of sensibility can be classed as a myth, a myth of the Fall. In this case the fall is from an organic society or culture into isolation, fragmenting and crippling division. To look back in this way to a lost golden age is a recurrent human activity. What distinguishes some of its modern forms (from, say, the mid eighteenth century on), is the locating of the golden age, the unfallen world, not in the never-never time of fairy tale or in the archetypal time of myth but in specific places and periods: in idyllic or uncorrupted primitive cultures (Tahiti, the Cossack tribes of the Caucasus or wherever); in a past phase of our own culture (early Greece, medieval Byzantium, Jacobean England or whenever). Those myths, Eliot's among them, that find their golden age not in a remote and primitive culture but in a sophisticated past era of our own can be seen as responding to an experience of the world that Matthew Arnold in the mid nineteenth century pronounced distinctively modern – the experience of one's world as bewilderingly, distractingly multiple, even inchoate. Such myths can be called in question and should, in my view, be decisively rejected – at least as dramatisings of the past which might actually illuminate that past (their possible function in the creative work of a Yeats or an Eliot or a Lawrence is another matter).

The first reason for rejecting Eliot's myth is that it is only one, if the most famous and perhaps the most elegant, myth of dissociation in early twentieth-century literary criticism and culture. The proliferation of such myths and the varying points at which they locate their Fall tells against their claims to historical validity [Kermode, in Roberts, 1975, pp.73–7]. Secondly, it does not particularly mesh with one's actual experience of Metaphysical poetry. It is far from clear what is meant by feeling one's thought as immediately as the odour of a rose and equally far from clear that Donne's poetry is characterised by such an activity. On the other hand, these formulations make good sense when viewed as the culmination of some tendencies in nineteenth-century French poetry and the criticism it inspired [Kermode, *passim*]. The combination of those two factors is decisive. Thirdly, dissociation of sensibility as a myth of cultural Fall is much too narrowly based in a purely literary history [cf. Eliot, 1957, pp.152–3]. Lastly, I would want to enter a general caveat: myths of a cultural Fall grow out of and feed into a cultural pessimism – in its milder forms nostalgic, in its darker doom-laden – about the present. There are usually grounds enough for being critical, even radically critical, of one's contemporary culture. To evoke the achievements of a past culture can articulate such criticisms. One rejects myths of a cultural Fall precisely because, being dramatic and absolute, they disrupt, if they do not short–circuit, that difficult double process of recognising the past as irreducibly *other* and, at the same time, bringing it to bear on the present.

Criticism since 1921

Eliot's revaluation of the Metaphysicals is meshed with his own activity as an innovating poet. The success of his revaluation may be meshed with larger changes in culture and society [cf. Everett, 1986, pp.34–5]. Such revaluations, as I said, have occurred before. What is new in the 1920s and after is that this revaluation coincides with a major expansion of the institutional study of English. This means that the insights and polemics of poets are taken up and systematised, become embedded in school and university syllabuses, in academic journals and readers' guides. The vices natural to such an institutional study are the petrifying of controversial insights into dogma and, finally, cliché; and the silting up of commentary that is pedestrian or wildly irrelevant or, sometimes, both. (Anyone interested in a cabinet collection of all these vices can spend a happy hour with the introductions to Carey's anthology of Marvell criticism.) Against this can be set the quality (and variety) of much academic criticism and (on a more mundane level) the multiplication of anthologies that make the criticism available.

In what follows I have classed criticism under the headings of (1) analyses of the nature of Metaphysical poetry, (2) literary histories of it. The latter lie close to (3) studies of this poetry in historical context. These, in turn, subdivide according to the kind of context explored: religious, social, political; contexts in the history of art or of ideas. Over against them we can group (4) detailed readings of individual poets though much of the best work in the study of contexts has been done when individual poets have provided the focus (e.g. Marvell and mid-seventeenth-century politics). To these we may add some anthologies and editions. Two of the best introductions to Metaphysical poetry are given by Grierson [1921] and Gardner [1957, 1967] in their respective anthologies. The former is an admirable example of an old-style literary history, moving freely across a wide range of literature to place and compare. Gardner concentrates more on analysing the basic features of Metaphysical poetry. At moments the analysis feels rather desultory but it remains a good place from which to get a first grasp of what Metaphysical poetry aims at.

Analytic accounts

The finest of these is probably Robert Ellrodt's *Les Poètes métaphysiques anglais*. This is unhappily still untranslated; readers without French can sample Ellrodt's approach in his chapter on 'Herbert and the Religious Poets' in Ricks [1970, pp.173–205]. James Smith [in Leavis, 1968 pp.157–71] claims that some of these poets are genuinely metaphysical and seeks to isolate how and when. He takes metaphysics to be characterised less by the answers it achieves than by the way it pursues them and the questions that prompt its pursuit. These are the questions raised by the experience of a fundamental reality of which mutually exclusive accounts can be given and yet the accounts seem valid and must be held in tension [pp.160–1]. Such a tension is maintained by the metaphysical conceit as Smith defines it. The elements of the conceit are 'such that they can enter into a solid union and, at the same time, maintain their separate and warring identity' [p.167]. He distinguishes this sharply from mere extravagant comparisons or from the hasty identifying of opposites he attributes to the poetry of Shelley; the essay closes with some glancing suggestions on the conditions in which metaphysical poetry can arise.

Smith's account is elegant and spare; perhaps too spare. One feels that it fingers something that is important, even crucial, to *some* Metaphysical poems. But that is its limitation: it is too abstract, too rarefied. Not only is there much Metaphysical poetry it will not cover but it isolates one feature from others no less crucial, such as rhythm, where Empson [1953] brilliantly evokes and integrates the different aspects of the poems he analyses.

His analyses occur in the course of an enquiry into the workings of ambiguity in poetry but can largely be read independently of this. They are carried out with great verve, paraphrasing exuberantly and sometimes laced with Freudian psychology (notoriously at the climax of his account of Herbert's *The Sacrifice* [p.232]). They sometimes heap up alternative meanings that obfuscate rather than illuminate the poem (as with Donne's 'A Valediction: of Weeping' [pp.139–45]. But much of the splendour of *Seven Types* comes from the sudden switch of such analysis into reverberating generalisation (as with, for example, the comparison of Crashaw and Dryden [pp.218–220]). Much of it too comes from the swiftness with which the distinctive rhythm or style of a particular poem is seized in a memorable paragraph or phrase (e.g. on Donne's 'Apparition' [pp.146–7] or Herbert's 'Pilgrimage' [pp.129–30]); or from the long perspectives opened up in the account of 'dissolved conceits' that reaches from Vaughan and Marvell to Swinburne [pp.163–75].

Literary history

Introducing the volume of the *Sphere History of Literature in the English Language* which takes in the Metaphysicals, Christopher Ricks distinguishes *literary criticism* (which deals with *texts*) from *literary history* (which deals with *contexts*). This proposes too neat a division. Contexts (as their etymology – con-texts – implies) exist in varying degrees of closeness to and mesh with texts. Literary histories may attend, sometimes intensively, to individual works although their concern is with the individual work or author in relation to a larger field. They may work with organising concepts – 'the plain style', 'the line of wit' – that both describe and evaluate. It is through such concepts that they develop their case about which writers are important and why, what the significant patterns in a given field are, be it the rise of the novel or the Renaissance lyric. It is through such concepts that literary history reaches beyond a mere chronicle of dates and titles to map a field and pursue connections.

For past literature, as Eliot's famous early essay on 'Tradition and the Individual Talent' insists, does not constitute an order permanently fixed. Its order is altered by new work in the present [Eliot, 1952, p.15]; and it is from a standpoint in the present that literary history, like all other history, is written. The value of literary histories is in proportion to the clarity and comprehensiveness of their mapping and the illuminating power of the connections they make. These qualities, however, are likely to be in conflict. Comprehensiveness may forfeit clarity; the power to illuminate may be won at the price of one-sidedness and exclusion. Hence the best literary histories are often polemical and sometimes perverse (Leavis's *Revaluation*, C.S. Lewis's *English Literature in the Sixteenth Century*). Their value is not least when they provoke us to creative dissent.

Grierson in his Metaphysicals anthology introduction sketches contexts in both history and literary history. In the former he places Donne as a poet of Catholic background or indicates the importance for him and for his Cavalier followers of the Court. In the latter he groups and discriminates, making connections with the 'metaphysical strain' of medieval Italian poetry, connections between the style of Donne and the later Shakespeare, and contrasts between Donne and his followers, both secular and religious.

The most incisive literary histories to take in the Metaphysicals since Grierson are by Leavis [1936] and Yvor Winters [1967]. Both illustrate crisply the role of organising concept and specific judgement in literary history. In both literary judgements are interwoven with wider judgements about styles of culture and morality.

Leavis writes, combatively, in the wake of Eliot's essays on the Metaphysicals but his densely woven account offers a more comprehensive mapping and sharper distinctions. It groups Jonson with Donne as the founders of a tradition that runs through the court poets of Charles I's reign and Marvell, is lost in the literature of the Restoration but returns as a key element in the complex achievement of Pope. It is a tradition characterised by an urbane grace that can co-exist with a sinewy strength and expresses the complex values of a ripe civilisation [pp.15-36].

It can be argued that Leavis overvalues a minor poet like Carew at the expense of other poets at least as interesting; and though his case against Dryden is persuasive as far as it goes some of what is best in the latter (especially his translations) is ignored. One might claim too that Dryden remains a more important figure in Pope's background than Marvell. (In the passages Leavis quotes to enforce the connections between the last two the affinities seem, at best, tenuous [pp.28–9].) More generally this account can be challenged as idealising the culture inferred from the poetry of Jonson and Carew and the challenge might involve making a different group of writers central to this period.

Winters gives a quite different mapping, founded on the claim that the short poems of the writers in what he calls the plain style are the major achievement of English Renaissance poetry. His definition of the plain style [1967, p.4] is chiselled and suggestive and one value of his account is the challenge it offers to traditional readings of the period, displacing the poets of the courtly and Petrarchan style such as Sidney and Spenser in favour of his plain style writers who include both recognised major figures like Jonson and neglected ones like Gascoigne and Ralegh. It cuts across divisions of Elizabethan and Metaphysical and comes at the Metaphysical poets it claims for the plain style, such as Donne and Herbert, from a new angle. On the other hand, some of the claims for particular poems (e.g. the 'extraordinary polish' he finds in the Lord Vaux poem quoted on p.14) are preposterous; and they are asserted with a flatness that can only call out (in a way that Leavis does not) a rejection equally flat. In fact some of Winters's claims for individual poems (e.g. those of Greville) are highly persuasive. The question then becomes how far the extravagant individual judgements damage the overall mapping. It is a mapping, in any case, that probably illuminates other areas of Renaissance poetry more than it does the Metaphysicals.

Studies of context

Literary histories provide a transition to studies that seek to set literature in the context of other kinds of history: the history of ideas, of art, of religion and of politics.

Such studies may be organised around a single motif like Maren-Sofie Røstvig's [1954] which pursues the theme of rural retreat launched in a famous epode by Horace and still being quarried and refined by poets like Vaughan and Marvell. Or they may range as widely as Rosalie Colie's examination [1966] of paradox as an issue in philosophy and as a literary form.

CRITICISM SINCE 1921   31

They would take in studies of the impress of religious history on literature, like Louis Martz' pioneering exploration [1954] of how techniques of religious meditation are assimilated by poets of the period and Barbara Lewalski's heavily documented argument [1979] for the shaping of the seventeenth-century religious lyric by Protestant attitudes to the Bible and the Protestant paradigm of salvation. The relation of literature to the visual arts can focus on a single form like the emblem or a larger cultural phenomenon like the baroque. For the former Rosemary Freeman [1948] gives an adequate survey which can be supplemented by Mario Praz [1939]. For the latter there is a welter of studies to which Skrine [1978] or Warnke [1972] will offer an introduction. Scoular [1965] ranges out suggestively from a central concept of wonder to topics as varied as religious meditation and Renaissance interest in the small scale both in nature and in art.

All of these incorporate accounts of individual poets within a larger general study. But the exploration of context can equally be pursued from within the detailed study of an individual poet. The sketches of baroque art and emblem literature in Warren [1939] remain crisp introductions; Strier [1983] invokes Reformed theology to interpret Herbert and work on the interaction of Metaphysical poetry with politics naturally focuses on Marvell.

Readings of individual poets

(a) Donne. The enthusiasm for Donne in the 1920s revival of Metaphysical poetry yielded less good criticism than one might have expected and he still has not had the concentrated attention bestowed on Herbert over the past decade or the repeated attempts to fix and define the quicksilver talent of Marvell. His exaltation evoked two eloquently perverse attacks from J.E.V. Crofts and C.S. Lewis (in Gardner [1962, pp.77–89 and 90–9] respectively; the Lewis also in Keast [1962, pp.92–110] with the reply by Joan Bennett [pp.111–31]). Both (Crofts especially) read extravagant pieces as serious statement and crowd different kinds of poem together with what seems a wilful disregard of style and tone. But Crofts at least mounts his onslaught with a pugnacious elegance and Lewis can raise an objection worth meditating as when he claims: 'Donne's poetry is too simple to satisfy. Its complexity is all on the surface – an intellectual and fully conscious

complexity that we soon come to the end of' [Keast p.106]. The
essay as a whole, however, displays some of the less attractive
features of Lewis's criticism: rhetorical manipulation and the
slanting of evidence that goes with it [Keast, pp.98–9]; for rhetorical manipulation, see for example the description of Donne as
a 'parasitic' poet [on p.107] or the massing of quotations [on
pp.104–5]. His Donne writes not *about*, but *in*, 'a chaos of violent
and transitory passions'; 'the love of hatred and the hate of love is
the main, though not the only, theme of the *Songs and Sonnets*';
and poems which do not fit this account are classed as few and
exceptional [pp.106,104,103].

J.B. Leishman [1951] rebuts both Crofts and Lewis, pointing
out sensibly (if at excessive length) the strong element of play
and drama in Donne [e.g. p.90], the extravagance out of which
the drama can grow [e.g. pp.80 and 157]. Other poets are invoked
to define the distinctive quality of Donne; sometimes for straightforward comparison, sometimes, as in his interplay of Donne with
Jonson, more suggestively [e.g. p.28; cf. pp.213–17]. Leishman's
exposition is easy-paced, often ambling. He can use terms like
'poetical' with a startling haziness [e.g. p.137]; but he can also
offer a useful general direction like 'the meaning of Donne's poems
lies far more in the interplay between their logical structure and
their rhythm and cadences than in their occasional illustrative
imagery' [p.202] and follow it out firmly [pp.228–41]. Or he can
generalise effectively on the treatment of love as an end in itself
in the *Songs and Sonnets* [pp.14–17].

Sanders [1972] concentrates on the close reading of individual
poems. He deliberately ignores other critics except for Coleridge
in his marginal notes and Johnson whose critique he takes as a
starting point, rightly thinking it sets a challenge that all high
claims for Donne must meet. The close reading readily swells
into paraphrase [e.g. pp.68–74 and cf. the comment on pp.87–8]
that can end up blunting the poems. The best things in the
book are less the individual readings than Sanders's sensitivity
to Donne's irony (and to its dangers) [e.g. pp.50–6 and 144; cf.
on role-playing, pp.44–50] and his determination to discriminate
between what he judges classic in Donne and what inferior. This
is seen at its best in his account of the religious poetry. It is
organised around the concept of wonder and uses passages from
Lawrence and Wordsworth as touchstones [pp.111f], though it
involves playing down the poems' theology.

Carey [1981], as his title implies, seeks to connect Donne's biography, his poetry and the larger habits of mind and intellectual activity of which the poetry is a part-expression. He brings to Donne a zest for jagged and eccentric detail [e.g. pp.251 and 273] and a sympathy for zig-zag imaginings. He expounds briskly the proto-Dickensian elements in Donne [e.g. pp.136–47 or 274] and persuasively reclaims neglected poems like the unfinished *Progress of the Soul* [pp.148-59] or the lesbian Elegy 'Sappho to Philaneis' [270–1].

The biography stresses Donne's Catholic background, his frustrated ambition and his angling for place and patronage. Here, though, the briskness of Carey's approach plunges into a swashbuckling that simplifies and crudens. He claims that 'though he forsook the Roman Church he.never, in a sense, escaped its grasp. It remained close to his mind as a reproach or a threat, or as an adversary with which he hoped he might finally be reconciled' [p.35]. The opening chapter is titled 'Apostasy' and the next traces the impress of this claimed apostasy on some of Donne's poetry. It is unquestionable that his writing continues to show signs of his Catholic upbringing. But not all sixteenth-century converts from Catholicism felt themselves to have apostasised and certainly Carey's finding of the impact of this apostasy in the poems proceeds with a recurrent use of 'perhaps', 'must', 'at all events' [pp.25, 26, 32, 38 and 40].

A steamroller insistence on Donne's ambition and its unattractive features leads into a chapter on 'The Art of Ambition' which gives a disappointingly one-track reading of some lyrics [pp.108-12]. This, however, is as nothing to the extravagance of its version of Elegy 19 [pp.105-6]. The sadism Carey attributes to this poem 'finds a natural home in the sermons' [p.124]. In his account of the latter selective quotation can be deftly massed to build up a simulacrum of Donne as a lurid rhetorician [pp.122-5 and 133-4] that ends up at some considerable distance from the actual Donne – sometimes more humdrum, often more probing and sensitive – of the sermons. The excellent final chapter on 'Imagined Corners', on the other hand, gathers up the earlier studies of Donne's response to such phenomena as bodies, change, growth and death. It ranges through the focal images of the poetry to map the workings of his imagination in a fashion at once exhilarating and precise.

The relations of Donne, as poet and as a worldly and

ambitious man, to his social and historical context are handled with much more finesse in Barbara Everett's 'Donne: A London Poet' [1986, pp.1–31]. The concept of him as a London poet 'our first (perhaps our only) real master of the poetry of urban anxiety' [p.12] opens up a ranging discussion of his work and some of his styles [pp.13-25]. It illuminates both such features as Donne's 'extreme awareness of himself in relation to a surrounding audience' and also the obliquity and distancing devices of such an unmetropolitan-seeming poem as 'The Ecstasy' [pp.25–31].

A.J. Smith's study [1964] of the *Songs and Sonnets*, though sometimes overcrowded in its writing, brings out well Donne's mastery of syntax and rhetoric [e.g. pp.37-46]. It signals rapidly but precisely Donne's relation to traditions of European love poetry [e.g. pp.9–15]. Such relations can be pursued at more length in Guss [1966] for the Petrarchan tradition, in Helen Gardner's essay on 'The Ecstasy' (in Roberts [1975, pp.239–58]) for the Neo-Platonic tradition and in Smith's own later study [1985] of Renaissance love poetry for both.

(b)   Herbert. Herbert criticism has burgeoned in the last fifteen years. An older view saw him as a devotional poet in a limiting sense: charming, cosy, a trifle stuffy (e.g.Grierson [1925, p.150]). This has been largely shouldered aside by an increasing emphasis on Herbert as a major poet, unrestingly subtle and intensely self-aware. Eliot's changing judgements can be taken as an index of the overall shift. He moves from classing him as a minor poet of a special and limited awareness [1951, p.391] through the later rejection of that placing [1957, pp.45–6] to valuing him for 'his restless exploration of variety and . . .a kind of gaiety of spirit, a joy in composition' [1962, p.31].

J.H. Summers's *George Herbert: His Religion and Art* was the first overall study and remains an excellent survey. Its first three chapters sketch changing estimates of Herbert as a poet, his life and his religious milieu. The next three deal with the importance of form for Herbert, his views on language and his concern with hieroglyphs. The hieroglyph is defined as 'a figure, device or sign having some hidden meaning'. Summers aims to disperse modern misunderstandings which see hieroglyphic poems as unredeemably quaint. So in his chapter on the latter he moves from Herbert poems which meditate on the hieroglyphs found in nature, art or the Church to poems like 'Church-Monuments' which are themselves hieroglyphs to take in, finally, those, like 'The Altar', which are visual hieroglyphs. Their defensive and explanatory purpose may limit those chapters as may also too general a use of concepts like form. The closing chapters on 'Verse and Speech' and on Herbert's use of allegory and sonnet, by contrast, signal persuasively the variety of voices to be found in *The Temple* and Herbert's inventiveness within a traditional mode and a traditional form.

M.E. Rickey [1966] studies Herbert's word-play and revisions and the impulses at work in his religious attitudes and discipline which drive his poetry towards a minimalist art if not towards a final silence [e.g. pp.112f]. Helen Vendler [1975] gives a detailed reading of individual poems, beginning with a fifteen-page account of 'Vertue' and attending to the different kinds of poem in *The Temple*. 'One of the particular virtues of Herbert's poetry', she says, 'is its provisional quality' [p.25] and she deploys with a brilliant sensitivity the insights to be won from a study of what she calls 'the reinvented poem': the rewriting and redirecting carried out by Herbert within the changing course of many of his poems ([pp.25–56]; cf. the later chapter on 'Imitators and Adapters' [pp.100–36]).

Vendler comes to the fluidity of Herbert's poems through a sensitive detailed reading of them. The two studies by Stanley Fish [1972, 1978] explore similar effects more single-mindedly. A reader of the first should perhaps begin with the appendix 'Literature in the Reader', which proposes to shift critical attention from the work as object to the experience of the reader responding to the work. The opening chapter draws on Plato and Augustine to contrast two kinds of writing: the rhetorical and the dialectical. The former aims to confirm the reader in positions already held, the latter to bring about a radical transformation of the reader's self and perception. Such a writing is itself to be *used up*; it is a self-consuming artifact in the double sense specified by Fish [p.3]. Applied to Herbert this leads to extravagances seen at their worst in the initial comments on 'The Flower': 'to stop saying amiss is not only to stop distinguishing "this" from "that", but to stop distinguishing oneself from God' [p.157,cf.p.173]. This is wholly implausible as a reading of the poem and as theology. Elsewhere, however, Fish can give perceptive readings of particular poems and he meets the objection that this is simply a Herbertian trick with the significant question: 'where exactly does the poem live, on the page or in experience?' [p.202; cf. pp.203, 207].

Fish's reading can perceptively elucidate one kind of Herbert poem or strategy (cf.the status he gives 'The Holdfast' [p.176]) but will do little with others. And even with those poems where it does apply overstatement lessens or ignores the interaction between God and man that draws some Herbert poems taut.

His second study starts from the split or impasse that has developed in readings of Herbert between those which present him as a serene and stable religious poet and those which see him as restless, endlessly revising. Fish suggests that an answer may lie in the activity of catechising which he proposes as a model of how *The Temple* works. In catechising the teacher questions the pupil in such a way that the latter finds the answers for himself (see [pp.11–27]; also [pp.42–8] for distinctively Christian forms of catechising). This matches the relation of Herbert the poet to his readers [p.27]. The temple of his title is a spiritual temple created by the poems 'not on the page or in space, but in the heart of the reader' [p.54]. But at the end Fish – very deliberately – insists that his approach, like all others in his view, only returns us to the central contradiction which exists at the heart of Herbert's work, 'the contradiction between the injunction to do work . . . and the realization, everywhere insisted upon, that the work has already been done' [p.169].

The contradiction Fish explores here reaches back into theological issues and these are the focus for those readings which claim Herbert as a strongly Protestant poet.

The older studies by Martz [1954] and Tuve [1952] relate him to medieval liturgy and typology [Tuve] or to contemporary Catholic styles of meditation and devotion [Martz]. (Typology is a way of reading the Bible – more accurately specific areas of the Bible – which sees certain events and figures in the Old Testament as prefiguring events and figures in the life of Christ or of the Christian Church. Thus the exodus of the Israelites from their bondage in Egypt is seen as prefiguring the deliverance wrought by Christ from the bondage of sin. Typology occurs in the New Testament itself; it enjoyed a luxuriant development in later exegesis of the Bible and Christian theology and has interested some modern theologians and exegetes.)

Tuve urges sharply, against critics like Empson, the importance of reading a poet in the context of the traditions on which he draws. In the case of Herbert she holds these are the traditions of medieval liturgy and typology. She demonstrates convincingly the medieval antecedents of a poem like *The Sacrifice* and the range of reference Herbert poems (sometimes unpromising Herbert poems) can have. There is a danger, however, of the poems disappearing behind the documentation; what one comes to register is the poetry of the typology itself, not the Herbert poem in which typology is a working element. This goes with other features of Tuve's approach: a proliferating of details that sometimes outruns relevance [e.g. pp.89–90]; an idealising of the integrated world of meaning available to a poet in Herbert's tradition [e.g. p.103]; an overstressing of metaphor as a poet's means of creating meaning [e.g. p.182].

Tuve's Herbert is strongly affiliated to medieval Christianity. Much recent work has argued for a Herbert no less strongly Protestant. This Herbert is shaped by distinctively Protestant ways of reading the Bible; he engages with the doctrines of divine grace classically formulated by Augustine in the late fourth and early fifth centuries and revived, if not intensified, in the work of the major Protestant Reformers. Such readings can be sampled in Bell (in Roberts [1979, pp.63-83]). Strier [1983] systematically presents Herbert in relation to the radical insights of the Reformation; he sees him as adhering to these in the context of moves away from them in early seventeenth-century Protestantism [pp.84–113] and even as having affinities with religious radicals later in the century [174–5; cf.198–205]. His readings of individual poems interlace verbal and theological analyses (see e.g. his readings [pp.116–33] of 'Justice' (II) and 'Aaron' which are developed partly in opposition to the humanistic readings offered by Vendler).

Two other works can round off this section. Bloch [1985] concentrates on Herbert's (distinctively Protestant) ways of reading Scripture. Nuttall [1980] pursues some of the problems – of infinite regress and of a radically inhumane concept of God – raised by an Augustinian theology of grace with an elegant energy [e.g. pp.4–19] that occasionally degenerates into undergraduate bumptiousness [e.g. p.33].

(c) Vaughan. Herbert's disciple Vaughan can seem a marginal figure among the Metaphysicals – marginal if not eccentric or an odd man out. In the nineteenth century he was seen (and valued) as a kind of proto-Wordsworth. This was mistaken but perhaps not entirely so. That at least is suggested by Empson's acute

comments [1953, pp.174–5]. Rachel Trickett argues a careful case
for his affinities with, as well as differences from, Wordsworth and
the sense in which Vaughan might be considered a visionary poet
[Rudrum, 1987, pp.264–77] as does Michael Bird in a suggestive
if overwritten piece [ibid, pp.278–97].

Vaughan can also seem marginal or eccentric on account
of his involvement with Hermeticism. This system of thought,
a blend of religious philosophy, mysticism and alchemy, takes
its name from a collection of treatises written in Greek but
supposedly embodying revelations from the Egyptian God Thoth,
named Hermes by the Greeks. They have been dated to early in
the Christian era but in the Renaissance were widely held to
embody a primeval wisdom and were influential in some currents
of Renaissance thought. Vaughan's twin brother Thomas was the
leading English exponent of Hermeticism in the mid seventeenth
century and his poetry is unquestionably influenced by it; the
controversial questions are – in what ways, and how far? L.C.
Martin (in Rudrum [1987, pp.59–67]) briefly sketches the history of the Hermetic writings and quotes parallels from them
to individual passages in Vaughan. A fuller account is given
by Holmes [1932], who feels that Vaughan 'always transmutes
his Hermetic tradition in some personal and intimate manner'
[p.37]; it becomes what she happily characterises as 'an intuitive
knowledge, like an inward sense of touch, directed towards the
objects of Nature' [p.40]. Pettet [1960] notes Hermetic phrases
and concepts in Vaughan but combats some of the more extensive
claims for its role in his poetry. It influences mainly his attitude
to nature [pp.77–84]: 'with a few exceptions . . . his best poems
are among the ones that show a minimum of hermetic influence'
[ibid]. Smith [1985] on the other hand, in his final chapter on the
Vaughans, sees Hermeticism as carrying a powerful vision of an
organic, anti-mechanistic universe. The question continues to be
contested and readers interested in its ramifications can consult
the articles mentioned in the Further Reading.

The first impression of Vaughan as odd-man-out among the
Metaphysicals is the starting point for Mahood's survey of his
sources, images and distinctive vision [Rudrum, 1987, pp.5–45]
which despite some speculative flights (e.g. on Vaughan's Welsh-
ness [pp.6–7]) and flowery writing [e.g. p.12] remains a good point
of entry. Rudrum [1981] sketches the life and gives a rather chatty
discussion of the poetry. He does, however, bring out Vaughan's

distinctive sense of nature, formulating it at one point as 'the
dynamic harmony produced by constant flux' [p.63], and expanding this into a discussion of Vaughan's poetry of potentiality and
transformation [pp.104f]. Pettet [1960] offers a detailed reading of four poems, prefaced by useful, if plodding, chapters on
Vaughan's use of the Bible, Herbert and Hermeticism. He has
numerous good comments: for example on Vaughan's imaginative
world [pp.9–11], on his 'habitual rhythm . . . a looser, longer-
breathed measure than Herbert's short, compact cadences' [p.54],
on tensions of rhythm and form and on the rhetorical strain in
Vaughan [pp.183–95]. Yet in the end they do not quite add up to
a good book. The reading of the poems tends to the diffuse and
to such testimonial-style summings-up as: 'in sum, the lyric is
most firmly organised, with wholeness, balance and continuity'
[p.126]. This may point to a larger limitation. Pettet analyses
the poetry too much under separate headings. His study does
not concentrate intensively enough either on individual poems
or on patterns of Vaughan's work as a whole.

Such concentration is strenuously supplied by the two recent
large studies of Post [1982] and Calhoun [1981]. These are fairly
demanding in style and in the concepts they deploy and neither
– Calhoun especially – is for the beginner. Both give prominence
to the impact of the Civil War and its aftermath on Vaughan
[Calhoun, pp.38–57; Post, pp.116–56] (cf.Hill [1985, pp.207–25],
on Vaughan [p.211] as 'a small Welsh squire . . . his loyalties primarily local'). Both Calhoun and Post draw on Vaughan's religious
prose to illuminate his response, as the poet of an underground
church, to those experiences. Both argue for continuity as well
as development between his secular and his religious verse. Both,
above all, read him in terms of literary models and of the literary
strategies he deploys.

Calhoun claims as Vaughan's principal model the lyric sequences, with their distinct kinds of development and coherence
[pp.10–12], that originate in Dante and Petrarch and reach
Vaughan through the English sonneteers [pp.17–35]. This is taken
up in the context of Hermetic medicine [pp.132ff] and of the
elegies in *Silex Scintillans I* [pp.162–73]; and it is capped by a reading of the latter in terms of liturgical sequence [pp.173–85]. The
patterning Calhoun finds can be overschematic (as in e.g. his
account of the relation between the two parts of *Silex Scintillans*
[pp.190–2]). But despite this, and even if one does not find the

overall case convincing, the analyses of Vaughan's style [e.g. pp.84–7] can be highly suggestive.

Post gives a reading of Vaughan's second secular volume *Olor Iscanus* in terms of a polarity between pastoral and elegy, the second puncturing the myth-making of the first. He explores the different voices in it and in *Silex Scintillans* [pp.45ff and 157ff]. He comments with precision on what Vaughan takes from Herbert in the handling of stanza form and opens this towards wider issues [pp.80-97]. His preoccupation with the self-conscious and the self-reflexive can lead him into overreading [e.g. p.53] as the concern for contemporary context leads to an implausible reading of 'The Night' [pp.201–11]. But the emphasis on the self-reflexive can also yield a suggestive account [pp.168–85] of some of Vaughan's polemical poems as pieces that can on occasion undergo their 'own rite of verbal purification'. And he can bring off formulations both elegant and suggestive such as (on *Olor Iscanus*): 'Pastoral empties into elegy and the poet is continually robbed of the opportunity to "muse" at ease. He inhabits the solitary extremes of the imagination rather than a world in which solitude prevails' [p.43]. Or (commenting on 'The World'): 'Vaughan's writings possess visionary interludes without ever attaining visionary status' [p.128].

(d) Crashaw. It is characteristic of Eliot that his brief 'Note on Richard Crashaw' should, almost in passing, formulate the three topics that preoccupy most later studies, and should do so more suggestively than several of them. The first is Crashaw's extravagance: his images, says Eliot, 'even when entirely preposterous . . . give a kind of intellectual pleasure – it is a deliberate conscious perversity of language, a perversity like that of the amazing and amazingly impressive interior of St. Peter's'. The (related) second is the question of the erotic in Crashaw: 'we feel at times that his passion for heavenly objects is imperfect because it is partly a substitute for human passion. It is not impure, but it is incomplete.' The third is the claim that Crashaw alone among the Metaphysicals is primarily a European baroque poet [1928, pp.123 and 125].

Crashaw's affinities with European baroque poetry are lavishly documented by Praz [1958]. Austin Warren's general survey [1939] is subtitled *A Study in Baroque Sensibility.* This remains something of a model of what such a survey should be with packed and lucid chapters on Crashaw's religious and historical milieu, on baroque art and the art of the emblem. He distributes his attention carefully across the whole range of the poetry, analysing formal features [pp.160f] but balancing this with suggestive generalisations on his symbolism and distinctive sensuousness [pp.178–93].

The twin topics of extravagance and the erotic in Crashaw are exuberantly lit up by Empson [1953, pp.116 and 217–24]. R.M. Adams (in Keast [1962, pp.264–79]) rides out from discussion of incongruity in Crashaw and Dylan Thomas into general questions of taste, bad taste and their arguable relativism [pp.264–7 and 277–9]. He urges aggressively that in Crashaw's poetry 'decorums wonderfully collide' [p.270]. It is essential to his imagery (e.g. its frequent fusion of mouths and wounds) that Crashaw does not gloss over the antipathy of the elements fused 'for to sense [the antipathy] is to sense the depths of the feelings that override it' [p.268]. 'If we resist the poet's imaginative unification of his feelings about Christ on the grounds that kissing wounds is unlovely and perverse . . .we may seem to quarrel with the poem's central point, that love of Christ includes all extremes and reconciles all contraries' [p.271]. This *may* be the point of the poem; but one can still ask how far such absolute reconciliation of extremes is possible and whether Crashaw's style is suited to persuade us of it. Not to mention that such quasi-theological justifications omit that element of conscious perversity of language that Eliot was surely right to single out in Crashaw – and to claim as giving 'a kind of intellectual pleasure'.

Any such emphases are combated at length by Bertanosco [1971]. He insists that Crashaw's extravagances have a conceptual and intellectual base [e.g. pp.10–11; cf.pp.118–20 and 129] and that images modern readers find distasteful can be regularly matched in the emblem-books on which his poetry draws [pp.28–33] (this might be thought only to push the problem back a stage). But Bertanosco raises an important issue, which has a wider relevance than to Crashaw alone, when he says that 'the lines which since the eighteenth century have so rigidly divided the sacred from the profane, the celestial from the lowly, the serious from the jocose, were just beginning to be drawn in Crashaw's time' [p.11]. This, however, is not followed though (see the brief remark on taste [p.19]). Elsewhere he valuably brings out the affinities and interchanges between Catholic and Protestant devotional literature in this period [pp.43–53], and links Crashaw to the style of meditation and piety developed by Francis de Sales [pp.55-90].

Though extravagant, Crashaw's poetry is highly stylised in its extravagance and repetitive in its imagery. This might make it seem naturally apt for systematic analysis such as is provided by Williams [1963] of its imagery and Rickey [1961] of its rhyme-patterns. The former does not escape the dangers of cataloguing images in isolation from their working in the totality of poems; the latter is much taken up with detailed listing, even tabulating, of rhyme patterns but can widen these in suggestive generalisations [e.g. pp.26, 41, 44, 61].

One set of Continental affinities is examined in more detail by Young [1982] although there has been a recent emphasis on Crashaw's Englishness. His contexts, it is claimed, are to be found in the Laudian movement within the 1630s Church of England and in his Cambridge college, Peterhouse, a Laudian stronghold during Crashaw's residence as a Fellow there. This is the burden of Healy's study [1986], though he says disappointingly little on specific poems. It is also urged in the collection of essays edited by Cooper [1979. e.g. p.i or pp.105–8]. Several of the contributors to the latter attend systematically to grammatical and stylistic features of Crashaw's work (e.g. Asals to his use of participles and metonymy [pp.35–9 and 43f]; Freer to reflexive patterns in his work, [pp.79–82 and 83–7]; Hilyard to oxymoron [pp.171–3 and 188]). And it is along those lines of more detailed attention to Crashaw's immediate contexts and to features of his style less noticeable than his imagery that critical analysis may advance.

(e) Marvell. Marvell is the most elusive and glancing of the Metaphysicals, the one who draws on the widest range of other poetry but also the one whose poetry is emphatically stamped by encounter with history and politics – and is not least elusive when it is. Criticism might, accordingly, be grouped into studies which seek to define one aspect or area of his art; studies which relate him to the literary traditions on which he draws; and studies which focus on his political writings and on their connections (or lack of connection) with his lyrics.

Not, of course, that these groupings can be neatly separated as, for example, the general surveys by Wilcher [1985] and Everett [1986, pp.32–71] demonstrate. The former offers a good introduction to Marvell's *oeuvre*. It briefly fills in contexts, whether literary (e.g.[pp.29–31] on pastoral) or contexts of cultural and political history [e.g. pp.4–10, 106–45]. He claims that central to Marvell's work is an alert awareness that conventions of genre constitute 'a way of enshrining a particular perspective on mankind's encounter with the world' and that 'every attempt to pin down some aspect of human experience in words will inevitably oversimplify the endless complexities of man's predicament' [p.13]. He goes on to examine Marvell's use of traditions, his habit 'of sliding one meaning over another, like two transparencies' [p.15], considering, for example the deployment of the conventions of Elizabethan lyric in 'The Gallery' [pp.25–9], the use of pastoral conventions to open up gaps between readers and the pastoral figures or within the pastoral world itself [pp.50–4] or the transition from innocence to experience in a context of Marvell's relation to the Cavalier lyric [pp.78–82].

Everett can deftly characterise such features of Marvell's poetry as its 'quality of enchanted self-enclosure', its penchant for the small scale and ironic [pp.37–40 and 68–71] but her survey centres on a long consideration of the *Horatian Ode*. She questions the division often made between Marvell's lyric poetry (seen as essentially private) and the public writing of his Cromwell poems and later satires. Arguing for subtle interconnections between the two areas of his work, she claims that 'the peculiar sense of scale' in some of the best lyrics comes from the fact that 'they cut deep into their age' [p.56]. This claim is pursued through illuminating generalisations on the nature of mid-seventeenth century political experience [pp.55–66] and on the cultural changes it embraces [pp.60–2].

Marvell's relations to literary tradition are more extensively explored by Kermode (in Wilding [1969 pp.125–40]), Leishman [1968], Colie [1970], Friedman [1970] among others. Leishman documents Marvell's borrowings from a range of poets, contemporary, Renaissance and classical. The book is rather diffuse and the effect is sometimes one of snowflake accumulation but it can crystallise in suggestive generalisations (e.g.[pp.20–8] on Marvell as an amateur/MS poet or [p.67] on the beauty which is 'often a kind of sublimated prettiness'). Colie concentrates on Marvell's use of genres, lucidly defined [pp.19–20 and 278], on his mixing [e.g. pp.19–22] and exhausting [e.g. p.57] of them. This leads up to the key formulation on what she calls his 'unfiguring' [p.79] and the study then proceeds to a detailed reading of 'The Garden' and *Upon Appleton House*.

An exchange between Brooks and Bush on the *Horatian Ode* [Wilding, pp.94–124] raises some issues about the historical reading of past literature, even if one may feel they do not take discussion very far. Wallace [1968] gives an elegant, detailed plotting of Marvell's political poetry in relation to the constitutional crisis and constitutional issues of the mid seventeenth century.

Ricks (in Patrides [1978, pp.108-35]) touches on Marvell and politics through attention to a key feature of his style, his attraction to 'the self-inwoven simile', 'a figure which both reconciles and opposes, in that it describes something both as itself and as something external to it which it could not possibly be' [p.109]. Ricks compares and contrasts Marvell's use of it with that of other writers from Donne to Meredith, and most interestingly with its use by the group of modern Ulster poets who write, as Marvell does, 'out of an imagination of civil war' [p.125]. A.J. Smith's essay in the same volume [pp.56-86] sees the experience of permanent tensions and frustrations as underlying Marvell's metaphysical wit: 'his poetry . . .gets its special power and quality from a distinctive apprehension, a kind of double or multiple vision realized in the wit' [p.86]. Finally Carey in the same volume [pp.36-54] pursues the poems' 'meticulous and intricate and often playful manufacture of reversed intentions and self-defeating activities with, over all, a potent feeling of constriction' [p.153]. He suggests possible causes for such a feeling in mid-seventeenth-century history and thought [ibid] but also in more general experience of what he calls 'reality's frustration mechanism': 'to know a thing you must name it; but once you have named it, it is no longer the thing you were trying to know' [p.139]. That recognition of an inherent irony in our relation to the world combines lucidity and a kind of dead-end resonance in a way that makes it (to my mind) a good stopping point for a survey of Marvell criticism.

Part Two: Appraisal

Metaphors far-fet[ched] hinder to be understood.

[Jonson]

Processions that lack high stilts have nothing that catches the eye.

[Yeats]

I take this cadence from a man named Yeats;
I take it and I give it back again.

[Roethke]

Style: preliminary definitions

Style is, notoriously, an elusive term. Buffon's 'Style is the man himself', like other epigrammatic definitions, may be suggestive but is too brief to take us very far. It does, however, crystallise one sense in which the term is used: style as personal, the quality that signs a writer's work as individually *theirs*. 'If you met those lines running wild in the deserts of Arabia', said Coleridge, after quoting some Wordsworth, 'you would immediately exclaim "Wordsworth"!' Opposed to this is the sense of style as anonymous, as belonging to a form and not to any one writer within that form. So we can speak of a ballad style or the style, self-consciously laconic, of the medieval Norse sagas. Such a style may seem close to, and yet must be distinguished from, what we may call the high impersonal styles in which any sense of individual utterance has been purged, where it seems as if a situation were uttering itself in language without human fashioning at all. Yet at such moments (e.g. the end of *King Lear* or of Wordsworth's *Michael*) there is no sense of the abstract or detached. Rather, the language has a quality at once bare and intensely charged; what is being presented is apprehended so intensely that any sense of presentation is swallowed up. Such a style is as remote as can be from style in a fourth sense in which it overlaps with stylishness: style as display, flamboyance, panache. I want to discuss the Metaphysicals in terms of style in yet another sense: style as historical, the style of a period or a school.

For styles are historical phenomena; they come into being in particular contexts, are transmitted, flourish, mutate, decay. It is this which enables an experienced reader to assign an unknown and anonymous passage to its probable period with some confidence. But I have not cited the other senses of style simply to clear the ground; we shall see that they all, even the third, bear at one point or another on the work of our poets.

As historical, styles are a form of memory, including – not least – the memory of the poet's own earlier work. Consciously or unconsciously, explicitly or implicitly, they carry a sense of the past – of what has been done, of where the present stands in relation to it, of what can, or needs to, or must, be done now. ('Style,' to shift a phrase of Barbara Everett's somewhat from its original focus, '*is* historical intelligence' [1986,p.129].) Obviously the degree to which poets are aware of this will vary. No less obviously the poet's sense of history, even if he is as learned a poet as Milton, will be highly specific and selective. It will be a sense of history in terms of ancestors, family relations, oppressive relatives and encounters with strangers – writers alien or remote who nonetheless speak, liberatingly, to him. So Eliot finds his own creativity released through the nineteenth-century French Symbolist poets and the Jacobean drama. (Cf. the engaging essay on 'What Dante Means to Me' in Eliot [1965, especially pp.126-7].) So the young Donne – and not he alone in the 1590s – finds models in the urban Latin poets of the first century, in the satirists Horace, Persius and Juvenal, and in the love-elegies of Ovid.

As historical, all styles, even the most idiosyncratic or impersonal, are generated in an interplay between the given and the made, the inherited and the freshly creative. The elements of the given and the inherited are most obvious in the forms that poets work. Less obvious but more fundamental and pervasive are the elements given by the basic features of a language or of a language at a given phase of its development. Readers of *1984* will recall the hapless poet Ampleforth who ends up in the cells of the Ministry of Love for the thoughtcrime of having retained the word 'God' in a Newspeak edition of Kipling's poems. 'It was impossible to change the line', he tells Winston, 'the rhyme was "rod". Do you realize that there are only twelve rhymes to "rod" in the entire language?' He adds: 'Has it ever occurred to you that the whole history of English poetry has been determined by the fact that the English language lacks rhymes?' Winston – not unreasonably in the circumstances – does not find this a particularly important or interesting thought. Yet such a feature of a language can be crucial to the development of a particular style. For a style can take its starting point from the conversion of such a limitation into a resource.

This is what occurs – classically – with Byron's taking up of the Italian ottava rima stanza in his late poetry. Because rhymes are much more abundant in Italian than in English and because double rhymes sound natural in Italian whereas, if used with any frequency at all, they sound comic or extravagant in English, the ottava rima, an eight-line stanza using only three rhymes, has had a long history as a maid-of-all-work in Italian poetry. In English it has been used for serious poetry by Chaucer, Keats and Yeats, but its most triumphant use has been by Byron who seized on the difficulty of finding natural-sounding rhymes for it over the stretch of a long poem and made that difficulty pivotal, as in this stanza from his first masterpiece in ottava rima, *Beppo*:

> But I am but a nameless sort of person,
> (A broken Dandy lately on my travels)
> And take for rhyme, to hook my rambling verse on,
> The first that Walker's Lexicon unravels,
> And when I can't find that, I put a worse on,
> Not caring as I ought for critics' cavils;
> I've half a mind to tumble down to prose,
> But verse is more in fashion – so here goes.

This happily mimes what it pretends to lament, the rhymes becoming more tumbledown as the stanza unrolls. The joke it conjures out of a difficulty becomes a starting point for the comic style – at once casual and acrobatic, continually dissolving and reforming expectation, disconcerting, melancholy, buoyant – of Byron's ottava rima poems.

Here the conversion of a form, and with it the genesis of a

style, occurs in the context of its transplanting from one language, one literature, to another. Equally, it can occur within the history of a literature. It can be a matter of a single strategic insight as with Empson's transformation of the villanelle. Or it can be built up over a stretch of time as with the rise of the heroic couplet in the later seventeenth century.

Originally used in medieval French pastoral poetry, the villanelle is an elaborate form – a nineteen-line poem, allowing only two rhymes and with two refrains introduced in the first stanza, alternating in each stanza thereafter and brought together at the close. Such rigidity would seem to fit it for displays of ingenuity more than anything else; or, at most, for a chiming, intricate elegance. And this is how it was practised by some minor poets of the 1890s, like W.E. Henley, among whom it and other elaborate medieval French forms enjoyed a certain fashion. Henley even wrote a villanelle on the form that plays on those limitations:

> A dainty thing's the villanelle
> Sly, musical, a jewel in rhyme,
> It serves its purpose passing well
>
> A double-clappered silver bell
> That must be made to clink in chime . . .

Empson puts the same limitations to very different effect in his 'Missing Dates':

> Slowly the poison the whole blood stream fills.
> It is not the effort nor the failure tires.
> The waste remains, the waste remains and kills.
>
> It is not your system or clear sight that mills
> Down small to the consequence a life requires;
> Slowly the poison the whole blood stream fills.
>
> They bled an old dog dry yet the exchange rills
> Of young dog blood gave but a month's desires.
> The waste remains, the waste remains and kills.
>
> It is the Chinese tombs and the slag hills
> Usurp the soil, and not the soil retires.
> Slowly the poison the whole blood stream fills.

Not to have fire is to be a skin that shrills.
The complete fire is death. From partial fires
The waste remains, the waste remains and kills.

It is the poems you have lost, the ills
From missing dates, at which the heart expires.
Slowly the poison the whole bloodstream fills.
The waste remains, the waste remains and kills.

He seizes on the villanelle's elaborate rigidity of form to articulate his urgent, sombre theme – the waste and loss inherent in human life; and in so articulating it the characteristic music of the form is converted from Henley's chime to this gong-beat of desolation.

The pentameter couplet, again, has been one of the central metres of English poetry since Chaucer. A distinct form of it, the heroic couplet, emerges in the mid seventeenth century and is carried to its final perfection it the early eighteenth by Pope. In this form each couplet is a self-contained unit of meaning, the rhyming is firm, if not emphatic, and there is a tendency to have a strong mid-line pause or a pause at the end of the first line. These characteristics build into the heroic couplet a capacity for balanced and epigrammatic statement, make it naturally apt to such figures of speech as antithesis, chiasmus and zeugma. So Pope brings off effects like:

> Sole judge of truth, in endless error hurled,
> The glory, jest and riddle of the world

or

> The fur that warms a monarch warmed a bear

or

> Damn with faint praise, assent with civil leer,
> And, without sneering, teach the rest to sneer.

A particular form generates, or opens itself to, particular figures of speech, a distinctive syntax and rhythm. These in turn work to define the meanings that the poet creates, his distinctive articulation of experience.

Style in the first sense listed above, style as personal, develops in interplay with impersonal poetic forms and with given features of a language. But it also develops in interplay with the voices of earlier poets taken as models or engaged with as masters. Talking in his essay 'Feeling into Words' of a writer's discovery of his own voice, the proper music of his poetry, Seamus Heaney asks:

> How then do you find it? In practise, you hear it coming from somebody else, you hear something in another writer's sounds that flows in through your ear and enters the echo-chamber of your head and delights your whole nervous system . . . This other writer, in fact, has spoken something essential to you, something you recognise instinctively as a true sounding of aspects of yourself and your experience. And your first steps as a writer will be to imitate, consciously or unconsciously, those sounds that flowed in, that in-fluence. [1984, p.44]

Here the relation of the poet to his predecessors is seen as creative, benign. But it is not always so. Predecessors can liberate: they can also crush or mislead; and the greater the predecessor the greater (perhaps) the danger. (It might be at least a half-truth to say that Shakespeare and Milton are the two greatest misfortunes of later English literature [cf. Eliot, 1957, pp.150-1].) The ways in which a major poet can prove baleful for those who come after vary. One occurs when he develops the possibilities of a style to a point at which no subsequent development seems possible. (Eliot records that Pound induced him to destroy a passage of Popean couplets in the draft of The Waste Land, saying 'Pope has done this so well that you cannot do it better; and if you mean this as a burlesque, you had better suppress it, for you cannot parody Pope unless you can write better verse than Pope – and you can't.')

This is one reason why styles die. It can be argued to be what happens to Metaphysical poetry with Marvell. One would expect it to happen late in the history of a style and it commonly does. But it can also happen much earlier, even when a style is first founded. Or so Carew suggests in his masterly elegy on Donne.

The pre-emptive founder? Carew's Donne

This appeared with other elegies in the first collected edition of Donne's poetry in 1633, two years after his death. Like Auden's 'In Memoriam W.B. Yeats' it pays its subject the tribute of an imitation that is salute and not pastiche. It puts into circulation some of the key counters (eventually the clichés) of later Donne criticism: 'his masculine expression', his 'imperious wit' (which the epitaph develops on lines that anticipate Coleridge), the myth or half-myth of Donne as a radical iconoclast, making a revolutionary break with contemporary poetry. But what makes Carew most suggestive as a critic of Donne is that his appreciation is entwined with a sense of literary history and of that history in turn as bound up with the history of language and culture.

The elegy carries a strong sense of English as a language for poetry at the time Carew writes – its possibilities, its limitations, the pressures upon it. It takes its place on this score among the debates on the status of the modern languages and of literature in them, over against classical Latin and Greek, which are a central phenomenon of the Renaissance – (see e.g. Jones [1953]). The recovery and editing of classical texts had been the grand achievement of Renaissance humanism. The humanist educational programme centred on them. But the very achievement of the classical writers posed a challenge to any modern literature: could it hope to equal them or was it condemned, in Carew's formula, to 'servile imitation' or:

> Licentious thefts, that make poetique rage
> A mimic fury, when our souls must be
> Possessed, or with Anacreon's ecstasy
> Or Pindar's, not their own.

These lines offer a range of negative images that counter the image of influence as creative offered by Heaney. And the damaging relation of modern to ancient is widened from individual poets to the languages in which they write:

> the subtle cheat
> Of sly exchanges, and the juggling feat
> Of two-edg'd words, or whatsoever wrong
> By ours was done the Greek or Latin tongue.

It is this displacement that Donne's achievement counters. Carew sees it as twofold. Donne has restored a balance between present and past ('Thou didst pay/ The debts of our penurious bankrupt age') and he has unclosed the resources of the English present for poets who come after him ('open'd Us a Mine/ Of rich and pregnant phansie, drawn a line/ Of masculine expression').

Yet a sense of cultural belatedness persists. Donne has to wrestle with a language less pliable and musically appealing than those of the classical poets. This is a fact about his historical position (and also about the common superficiality of human response that prefers such musical appeal. The recalcitrance of both factors is compacted in the sombre phrase 'the blind fate of language'). He also comes after they have culled 'the prime/ Buds of invention many a hundred yeare,/ And left the rifled fields'. In a triumphant hyperbolical turn Carew sees the second of these difficulties as only underscoring Donne's achievement and the first as helping to shape it:

> yet thou may'st claim
> From so great disadvantage greater fame,
> Since to the awe of thy imperious wit
> Our stubborn language bends, made only fit
> With her tough thick-ribbed hoops to gird about
> Thy giant fancy, which had proved too stout
> For their soft melting phrases.

Resistance masterfully overcome – this is what Carew picks out as essential to Donne's poetry. But the resistance is as essential as the mastery. It contains and orders a violent and hyperbolical imagination which, unresisted, would be merely overweening.

The corollary of this achievement for Carew is the demands it makes on poets who come after. It is on Donne's poetry as exclusive and exacting – impossibly exacting – that the final emphasis goes ('But thou art gone, and they strict lawes will be/ Too hard for Libertines in Poetrie').

Carew's sense of literary history includes a sense of its fluctuations, of achievements won against the odds and of how difficult, if not impossible, these achievements may be to transmit. Taking this a step further we can ask if the difficulty does not sometimes lie in the achievements themselves. It is not only the expelling of classical mythology as decoration that later poets (Carew among them) will be unable to match. It is the entire working of a poetry so imperious and so comprehensive. *Has* Donne opened a mine that later poets can work? Or, in founding a school, has he brought it about that its pupils can only be imitators?

A School of Donne?

But did he, indeed, found a school? If the term is taken to mean that the later Metaphysicals derive strictly from Donne it proves misleading or downright wrong. It proves misleading, firstly, because it runs counter to our initial experience. No one who comes to Vaughan from Donne is likely to feel after half an hour that he has been reading pretty much the same kind of poetry. If we suppose that all the Metaphysicals are like Donne we shall end up by distorting their work to make it match his or else taking his as a model that we blame them for failing to reach. The notion of a School of Donne is misleading, secondly, because Donne is so various. If it is said that a later poet follows Donne one should ask *which* Donne for there are several, and some of his most distinctive effects are not taken up by any poet who comes after. It is misleading, thirdly, because what Donne establishes is not a genre but a style.

A genre, as I use the term, is defined principally by *structural* conventions common to all specimens of the genre; to a lesser degree it is defined by a common subject-matter or field. Styles too work with conventions. But style defines the *texture* not the structure, of a work (though particular genres will carry styles broadly appropriate to them like the grave or high style of epic, the flamboyant style, shot with irony, of the Jacobean revenge play).

There may be a shared Metaphysical style but there are no structural features common to all Metaphysical poems, no paradigm which will define the essence of a Metaphysical poem – that which makes it a Metaphysical poem and not something else. If we try to catalogue the features common to all Metaphysical poems we shall end up either baffled or with a lowest common factor of small illuminating power. What may prove useful is to define some key features of a style forged by Donne in the context of the turbidly creative and experimental writing of the 1590s; to trace the history of that style as later poets imitate, assimilate or transform it; and to suggest some reasons why its history develops

as it does. In *this* context the term 'School of Donne' may illuminate if we think of its analogy with the term as employed by art
historians discussing, say, the school of Rubens or of Donatello,
where school speaks of a shared style and treatment of subjects,
of apprenticeship and techniques acquired and of the studio of
the master in which apprentices learn.

Donne: the founding of a style

The most immediately striking feature of the Metaphysical
style forged by Donne is its use of the conceit. The best
basic definition of the latter is given by Helen Gardner:

> a conceit is a comparison whose ingenuity is more striking
> than its justness, or, at least, more immediately striking. All
> comparisons discover likeness in things unlike: a comparison
> becomes a conceit when we are made to concede likeness while
> being strongly conscious of unlikeness. [Gardner, 1967, xxiii]

This sense of unlikeness means that the conceit always carries
an element of the extravagant, the playful. When unlikeness is
strenuously insisted on it gives the conceit a quality of cultivated
discord that brings it close to the grotesque. (For some readers
– Johnson among them – Metaphysical conceits simply *are* grotesque.) It shares with the grotesque at large a power to arrest
attention by disrupting, by enforcing connections across what
seem natural divisions. One context, indeed, for the Metaphysical
poetry of the conceit may be found in the sudden florescence of
the grotesque that occurs in the writing of the 1590s. But the drive
of the conceit to map and analyse experience separates it from the
grotesque. Donne's *Satires* and *Elegies* crackle with an intermittent
energy of the grotesque but it remains a matter of extravagant
physical detail, a relish for the distorted and the overblown that
sometimes turns nasty. This kind of imagining can be taken up
and purified in lyric. The song 'Goe, and catch a falling starre'
cultivates discords that have not taken on the fixity, still less the
ordering power, of the conceit. It plays off its chanted fairy-tale
impossibilities against a brash cynicism but remains a poem of
beautifully interlaced incongruities that stop short on this side
of conceits.

In 'Love's Growth', by contrast, conceit works with analogy and metaphor to articulate a meditation on love as seasonal, inescapably bonded to the cycle of nature. The first stanza mockingly recognises that love *is* seasonal: 'Methinks I lied all winter, when I swore,/ My love was infinite, if spring make it more'. The second counters this in a delicate interplay between analogies that simply clarify a point:

> not greater, but more eminent,
> Love by the spring is grown;
> As, in the firmament,
> Stars by the sun are not enlarged, but shown,

and metaphors that integrate the items they bring together:

> Gentle love deeds, as blossoms on a bough,
> From love's awakened root do bud out now.

In the next four lines analogy does not only illustrate; it suffuses the development of the thought with an ordering calm and by the end we have passed from analogy to full conceit:

> If, as in water stirred more circles be
> Produced by one, love such additions take,
> Those like so many spheres, but one heaven make,
> For, they are all concentric unto thee.

There is a movement, instantaneous but not abrupt, from ripples in water to the astronomical spheres on which, in the old cosmology, the planets were carried, and the final effect is of a closing up that is at once intellectually elegant and a deeply felt compliment. In the closing lines a conceit works rather differently:

> And though each spring do add to love new heat,
> As princes do in times of action get
> New taxes, and remit them not in peace.

Here the parenthetic comparison has an effect of deliberate discord, sharpened by its snappier rhythm and tone of sardonic worldly wisdom. It makes a sharp break with the poem's fundamental stress on love as natural; but in so doing it redirects our response so that we are readied for the serene transcendence of both naturalism and worldly wisdom in the final line:

> No winter shall abate the spring's increase.

Stepping back from these examples we can now formulate some general points about the working of the conceit. First, the conceit may be the most obtrusive feature of Metaphysical poetry but – in Donne at least, whatever may be true of a second-generation Metaphysical poet like Cleveland – it does not work in separation from other devices and energies of the poem. Secondly, the conceit belongs with, and readily passes into, other devices such as analogy and hyperbole. What it shares with analogy is a certain abstracting quality, a noting of correspond-ences which can be used to place the objects compared on some kind of intellectual graph. What separates it from straightforward analogy is its extravagance, its relishing of discord and its cultivation of surprise. These ally it with hyperbole and the hyperbole of the conceit is one element that gives Metaphysical poetry its widespread element of play. At its best this play is extravagant, intellectual and controlled. Because it is the last two of these it can also be, in its very extravagance, clinchingly neat. Its quality of play is the third element we can isolate in the con-ceit. (Not that Metaphysical hyperbole should be confined to play; it is also crucial to Donne's dramatising of, for example, situations where hyperbole seems the natural language of ecstasy, as in 'The Sun Rising,' or of desolation, as in the 'Nocturnal'.)

Conceits in the lyrics are a vehicle for argument as well as analysis; the two indeed can hardly be separated. One root of the latter lies in the Ovidian love poetry Donne imitates in his *Elegies* with its elaborate persuasions and casuistry. The charac-teristic tone of such argument is masterful, passing readily into the brutal. A very different style of argument – grave, intricate but not unvisited by irony – is rooted in Neo-Platonic traditions of the analysis of love. More general contexts are provided by the disciplines of theology and law, both of them professional – and more than professional – interests for Donne.

This account has deliberately focused on Donne's lyrics. It could be argued that the Metaphysical style is naturally suited to lyric and that the few notable long poems in this style (Donne's *Anniversaries*, Marvell's *Upon Appleton House*) are only freakishly successful at best; certainly Donne's lyrics, secular and religious, are his crowning achievement. A lyric is originally a poem written to be sung and all lyric might be said to occupy an area bracketed between song and speech. In that it moves towards song lyric concentrates and purifies experience. But the price it commonly pays for that concentration is the degree to which it must exclude and abstract. Donne's achievement in the *Songs and Sonnets* and in the *Holy Sonnets* and *Hymns* is to create a lyric poetry that welds speech-as-song with speech-as-drama and both with argument and with analysis, be the argument and the analysis intense, extravagant, jokey or dogged.

The achievement is not, of course, unique to Donne. One might say that the history of lyric poetry is contoured by precisely the attempt to achieve the intensities peculiar to lyric without sacrificing the fullness proper to other forms. Such fullness is sought by the grander forms of lyric such as the ode whether as practised by Pindar in Greek or Horace – one of Marvell's masters – in Latin or the English Romantic poets. In Renaissance literature it can be found not only in elaborated lyric forms like the canzone or epithalamium but in some sonnet-sequences.

The young Donne was sketched by a contemporary as 'not dissolute but very neat, a great frequenter of plays, a great visitor of ladies, a great writer of conceited verses'. The conceits we have touched on; his verse is dramatic in a number of interlocking ways. It is dramatic in the energy it gives to speech and in its famous explosive openings:

> When by thy scorn, O murderess, I am dead,
> And that thou think'st thee free
> From all solicitation from me,
> Then shall my ghost come to thy bed,
> And thee, feigned vestal, in worse arms shall see.
>
> ['The Apparition']

This is a kind of drama that is, zestfully, self-dramatising. It runs to the flamboyant and the histrionic ('What if this present were the world's last night?') There is a quieter drama that catches the twists and refluxes of thought or the shift and slide of a relationship within the situations that the openings so masterfully create. What Donne's drama never gives, of course, is the sense of other selves, objectively created and radically free of their creator, that we get in Chaucer's *Troilus and Criseyde* or in Shakespeare or some novelists. It is always a drama of the masterful, assertive, exploring *self*.

Nonetheless this dramatic quality brings into Donne's poetry a strong sense of multiplicity. On the directest level it creates a sense of the multiple roles a speaker might play. That feeds, on a deeper level, into a sense of the multiple potential selves that might wait within an individual to be realised. And beyond both lies a sense of the multiple perspectives in which an act or situation might be viewed.

The conceit and (perhaps) the drama can be linked to another feature of Metaphysical poetry less immediately striking but, I would argue, not less central – what we may call its miniaturising. By miniaturising I do *not* mean a cultivation of the exquisitely fragile or delicate or bijou. I mean an art for which concentration is central but one which concentrates, primarily, not by straining or distilling but by telescoping the large scale into the small; an art of the intensely circumscribed, of the englobingly tiny or complete. The converse of this is that the miniature in Metaphysical poetry is always potentially and sometimes actively distended by what it carries. It is always ready to open – sometimes not open but explode – into its opposite.

If we ask why miniaturising should be so prominent in this poetry, even central to it, a number of answers can be suggested. (They range, interestingly, through literary history proper into the history of culture and world-view at large.)

In English painting the late sixteenth and early seventeenth centuries are the great age of the miniature portrait. Donne, who had himself painted by Oliver and (probably) by Hilliard – the two leading English miniaturists – writes of the latter in 'The Storm': 'a hand, or eye/ By Hilliard drawn, is worth a history/ By a worse painter made'. This might be suggestive in its emphasis on the miniature's power to compress or imply. Donne's own 'Canonization' prefers 'a well-wrought urn' to 'half-acre tombs' and claims for its lovers that they 'did the whole world's soul contract, and drove/ Into the glasses of your eyes/ (So made such mirrors, and such spies,/ That they did all to you epitomize)'.

In literature several forms prominent in this period seek to encompass much in little. In the second chapter of her engaging book on genre in Renaissance literature Colie [1973] suggestively links several such forms: the adage and the essay, the epigram and the sonnet, and has a long discussion of the emblem – a form important for several of the Metaphysicals, notably Herbert and Marvell [pp.37–67].

The cultivation of the epigram in Renaissance poetry might also bear on Metaphysical miniaturising. Literally a poem to be inscribed on, as it might be, a monument or a statue, the epigram commonly carries a quality of concise and pointed statement. Its structure is designed to arrest attention and rouse curiosity which is then gratified in a single clinching stroke. Metaphysical poetry at large can be related to this vogue of the epigram [Gardner, 1967,xxii–iii] though it is the work of the non-Metaphysical Herrick that brings out most clearly the epigram's capacity to miniaturise.

A very different context can be found in the shift from a medieval to a modern cosmology. The universe, in the medieval model, is vast but *finite* with a hierarchic structure that encourages the making of analogies between microcosm and macrocosm. The decisive shift, which gets under way in the later medieval period itself and is not completed until the end of the seventeenth century, is from this closed world to an infinite universe.

The transition to a new model of the cosmos is driven by the major scientific developments of the sixteenth and seventeenth centuries in physics and astronomy. It is brought to a climax at the end of that period by the work of Newton. Pascal in his *Pensées* is perhaps the first sensibility to engage radically with the new cosmology and what it might mean for the human imagination and self-understanding. Pope is perhaps the last poet to deploy the old macrocosm-microcosm analogies while also taking the impact of the new cosmology. The brilliant use of scale-shifting that is central to his poetry is an index of his position between two worlds. Within the overall scientific movement such developments as the invention of the telescope and microscope obviously work more immediately to prompt a sense of drastically differing scales and of the possibility of moving between them. In this respect, as in others, Pope is the last major poet of a tradition that takes in Donne and Marvell.

The Metaphysical poets flourish in the period of transition when the closed hierarchical cosmos and the habits of analogical thinking that both helped to articulate it and were sustained by it have been radically undermined but not yet swept away. Those habits of thought and imagination can continue to operate but they are no longer rooted in a shared fundamental model of the universe. Because of this they can be practised with a flamboyant intensity since those who practise them do so without either the assurance or the responsibility of those who practise a mode of thinking that grounds or dominates their culture.

This leads into a final factor that belongs to social as well as literary history. Much Metaphysical poetry is exclusive while reaching towards inclusiveness. When secular it is often exclusive by its concentration on love as the experience of the world-excluding lovers (in contrast to the placing of erotic love in its context of society and of the controlling rhythms of nature and time that we get in Chaucer or in Shakespearean comedy and romance). In Donne this exclusion is upheld with a lordly extremism. In his Cavalier followers of the next generation it yields an insouciant poetry of flirtation. When religious, Metaphysical poetry is often exclusive in its devotional stances: in Donne again with an extremism but an extremism this time less lordly than willed (in some of the *Holy Sonnets*) or compelled (in the *Hymns*); in Herbert, Vaughan and Crashaw less intensely but no less thoroughly. Yet all the main Metaphysical poets except Crashaw are writers strongly responsive to the mundane world of politics, history and affairs even if excluded from it (unwillingly like Donne in his middle years or by conscious choice like Herbert at the end of his life). The miniaturising of their poetry transcends, or sometimes only straddles, the breach between their exclusiveness and their response to that larger world they exclude.

Groupings and generations

This account of the Metaphysical style has been deliberately weighted towards Donne; for Donne forges a complex new style and most of the poets we call Metaphysical define themselves in relation to him. Most but not all: Herbert, though connected to Donne by personal and family friendship, owes him little as a poet. The contemporaries who offer analogies for his work are Jonson and the Jesuit martyr Southwell. Its larger context is the movement, in the wake of Renaissance and Reformation, to create a dedicated religious poetry. In the next generation it is Herbert, not Donne, that Vaughan and Crashaw set out from, the former pervaded by him, the latter only grazed. When we come to look at the individual poets in some detail we shall see the configurations that the style analysed in the previous section takes in their work: how miniaturising, for instance, engages with the paradoxes of the Incarnation in Herbert or the experience of civil war in Marvell. But before doing so we can sketch in broader terms how the Metaphysical style develops in the generation after Donne.

Of his followers in that second generation Carew at his best elegantly skims off some surface effects of his style, Cleveland and Cowley, diversely, run it into the sand. Cowley does so by imitations which let Donne's effects peter out. Cleveland does so by isolating and intensifying a single feature of Donne's style – the conceit. 'What is the sign of every *literary decadence?*' asks Nietzsche in his polemic *The Case of Wagner* and answers:

That life no longer dwells in the whole. The word becomes sovereign and leaps out of the sentence, the sentence reaches out and obscures the meaning of the page, the page gains life at the expense of the whole – the whole is no longer a whole.

This seems a suggestive formulation as we move from Donne to his followers of the next two decades. His is a style hard to master or possess but all too easy to imitate. Particular features – the conceit, the argumentative tone – can be readily learned by an intelligent reader; to integrate them creatively is an achievement much harder won. Without such integration what were in Donne strategies of mastering and response become only techniques to be applied and finally tricks to display. The style he has created depends on the shifting, dynamic balance of a number of elements. If that balance is not maintained the style breaks up into its constituent elements and one of these can become dominant or exorbitant in the fashion Nietzsche diagnoses.

All styles in the end exhaust their resources, are shrivelled or stiffened by writers who reduce them to hand-down techniques or merely slide into their verbal habits. But the Metaphysical style is in danger of exhausting itself sooner than most. It does so, on the one hand, by the constant demands it makes, and, on the other, by its quality of engineered cleverness which makes individual devices comparatively easy to separate out and learn. Certainly of the poets who can be directly grouped as followers of Donne only Marvell and, to a lesser degree Lovelace, can be said creatively to develop the style they have learned. Herbert on this score proves the more fruitful master.

In addition to those preciser family groupings we can class all of the second-generation Metaphysicals – Cowley, Cleveland, Vaughan, Marvell and Crashaw with the Cavalier poets as outriders – together against the founding figures of Donne and Herbert. The differences between the generations can then be plotted as shifts within the traditions of an evolving style, shifts that bring both extension and loss. One clear loss is of the dramatic immediacy so vibrant in Donne. In Vaughan the openings that arrest us in earlier Metaphysical poetry have dwindled to a meditative scene-setting: 'I walkt the other day (to spend my hour)'. But this unemphatic entry that risks the ambling is bound up with the retirement and brooding out of which much of Vaughan's best poetry issues. In Crashaw drama is lost in baroque celebration. Marvell, refining to silhouette both the analytic drama of Donne and Herbert and the shadow-drama of flirtation in the Cavalier lyrists, deploys angular stances and poses liable at any moment to be overturned.

This slackening of the dramatic in the second-generation Metaphysicals can be related to the decline and final extinction of the stage drama (the public theatres were closed at the outbreak of the Civil War by the Parliament who controlled London; they did not open again till after the Restoration). It can be related more immediately to a diminishing of the analysis and argument which generate so much of the drama in Donne and Herbert. The diminishing of these, in turn, shifts the function and place of the conceit. It works less to analyse, map, master experience, becomes instead a largely self-contained entity. The miniaturising I have claimed as a key feature of the Metaphysical style is, if anything, heightened. But it lacks the comprehending or explosive power that miniaturising has in Herbert or Donne. It is devoted, rather, to creating microcosms of the extravagant.

Such development forks in two directions: it can lead, as in Cleveland, to a cord-knotting of ingenuities which makes the reading of the poem only the unpicking (and admiring) of these. Or it can lead, as in Crashaw, to a distending of the conceit, to glass-blown extravagances of which 'The Weeper' is the text-book example.

Such isolating and elaboration of the conceit co-exists with a development that in some ways runs counter to it: the shift from a poetry that in Donne is largely, in Herbert is almost entirely, stanzaic, to a poetry that is frequently on-running in the metrical forms that it uses. This is most emphatic when they use the octosyllabic couplet but even when writing in stanzaic forms Vaughan especially but also Crashaw and Marvell can override or absorb stanza frames in prolonged movements of syntax and rhythm. Conversely the fundamental unit of the poem in Vaughan and Crashaw (this would not be true of Marvell) is often not the sentence or the stanza but the phrase.

These are among the ways in which the Metaphysical style develops fruitfully after Donne. Having noted them it is natural to ask why they occur. One explanation would centre on issues of form. The achievement of Donne and Herbert as stanzaic poets could prompt a recognition (conscious or unconscious) in the poets who come after that, given the fertility of those two in the invention of stanza forms and virtuosity in their handling, no fruitful development beyond them was likely. Again, one might claim that as we move from Donne and Herbert to the poets of the second generation we find a displacement or decentring of the individual self, with its divisions, fluctuations and drama. Such a shift might be related, in turn, to larger-scale phenomena of mid-seventeenth-century culture and history: to the changing awareness of the cosmos touched on earlier; to the experience (in e.g. Vaughan, Lovelace, Marvell) of civil war; to the influence of particular styles of art or devotion (e.g. the baroque on Crashaw).

Donne

I ever did best when I had least truth for my subjects.

[Donne]

Donne: a 1590s Poet

Carew's image, in his elegy, of Donne as purging innovator is a myth in the sense that it simplifies and dramatises a complex historical situation. As good myths also do, it illuminates. Donne's innovating energy *is* extraordinary: it manifests itself alike in the rhythms of his verse, in the new forms he introduces and in the masterfulness with which he handles and crosses them.

He is one of the first writers of formal verse satires in English, the first considerable writer of verse-letters, the first writer of prose paradoxes and the first to imitate Ovid's love elegies in a vernacular language. But his very zest as an innovator links him to the context in which he begins to write, the context of the 1590s – arguably the central decade of English Renaissance literature.

I call it central because it has behind it the pioneer achievements of the writers of the 1580s which it can both refine and react against, and because it develops new styles and forms that reach forward into the seventeenth century. The 1580s had seen the opening up of a secular drama in the work of Marlowe and Kyd, the development of styles possessed of a new verbal glitter and a suppler rhetoric than that of the graver, more dogged, mid-century writers. These achievements are continued into the 1590s with the posthumous publication of Sidney's major poetry and prose and (1590, 1595) of the two main blocks of the *Faerie Queene*. What one might call the glass-and-ivory elegance of one Elizabethan style reaches its high point in Marlowe's *Hero and Leander* (posthumously published in 1598), in Shakespeare's *Venus and Adonis* and in some sonnet writing, most notably Shakespeare's own. In *A Midsummer Night's Dream* and in *Richard II* he puts such a style to more probing uses while the previous history plays, the three parts of *Henry VI* and *Richard III*, reach back to recall and extend (as Emrys Jones has argued in his *Origins of Shakespeare*) earlier Tudor material and styles.

The 1590s also see a range of new ventures: the beginnings of satire (as a distinct form), a new urban literature, a florescence of parody and the grotesque; and, of course, the rapid development of the drama. Its central writers are Shakespeare and the phosphorescent genius of Elizabethan prose, Thomas Nashe [Rhodes, 1980]. Both have a zest for verbal extravagance and parody. Both are virtuosos in the development of differing styles, in the intercutting of styles and in the effects of rapid, sometimes dizzying, change in perspective such intercutting can give.

These developments allow a marvellous combining of flexibility with intensity but they also carry their dangers. In Nashe multiplicity threatens to swirl into incoherence and the same threat may be there in early Shakespeare – one thinks of moments in the *Comedy of Errors* or *Venus and Adonis*. But in Shakespeare it is overcome by a mastery of juxtaposition and of framing devices.

By the time he is writing the *Henry IV* plays at the end of the decade he has brought those resources of parody and perspective to a point at which differing styles can be counterpointed with an elegant economy and with them the attitudes and responses they embody.

The dangers of incoherence for the writers of the 1590s are at their most obvious in verse satire and in the urban literature which overlaps with it. The latter projects an image of the city as a place of atomised crowds, of figures seen with the sharpness of caricature or silhouette; a scene pullulating with energy, confusion and sharp-witted cozening. The sense of multiplicity it can generate has a distinctive jagged edge and this is what we find eminently in Donne's *Satires*. It can also lead to fragmentation and disorder, not least in a satire so given to self-indulgent vehemence as is most satire of the English Renaissance.

Donne's *Satires* record his engagement with this teeming world which at once exhilarates and repels him. What saves them from incoherence is, firstly, a mastery of rhetorical syntax that works beneath and through their helter-skelter detail. The parentheses which multiply that detail can also isolate and lock it; accumulation can be ridden to a pounding climax; or it can be given a sudden, buoyant turn which allows Donne to *ride* his helter-skelter world.

The second feature that saves him from incoherence is the recurrent impulse towards the ideal of a centred stability and seclusion. It is the interaction of this with the satirist's gusto that gives Satire I its zig-zag vitality [cf. Everett, 1986, pp.3–8]. Both features foreshadow much in the later Donne. His exercise of control through rhythm and syntax (rather than, say, through structuring devices or imagery) bespeaks a writer intensely responsive to the immediate, a writer whose poetic voice takes naturally to the rhythms of speech and heightens them into rhetorical address, a writer attuned to drama who will end his career as a masterful preacher. The clamping down to lock and isolate detail occurs at a local level in much of the couplet verse of the *Elegies* and runs on into the *Anniversaries* of his middle years to be found at its most elaborate in the Chinese-boxing of his late religious prose in the *Devotions* and (sometimes) the sermons.

The impulse to withdraw into the self, the quest for some

centred stability, is more explicitly pursued, in his early poetry, by the verse-letters to his men friends. It can be glimpsed at moments in some of the earliest, like 'To Mr B.B.' or 'To Mr E.G.', which are less letters than post-cards in verse. In 'To Mr Rowland Woodward' ('Like one who in her third widowhood') it is knit into a complex process of inturning and outgoing. And in one of the letters to Sir Henry Wotton ('Sir, more than kisses') it becomes a sustained interplay of fixity and travel: 'Be then thine own home, and in thyself dwell;/ Inn anywhere, continuance maketh hell'.

That has behind it an exasperated satirist's sense of what is wrong with life in court, city or country crossed with a very different, a haunting, sense of the instability, the contingency of the human self in whichever of these it moves:

> I think if men, which in these places live
> Durst look for themselves, and themselves retrieve,
> They would like strangers greet themselves, seeing then
> Utopian youth, grown old Italian.

It is Satire 3 that grapples most strenuously with those issues, lifting the quest for a centring stability into the winding ascent of the famous central lines: 'On a huge hill/ Cragged, and steep, Truth stands, and he that will/ Reach her, about must, and about must go'. And at the end of the poem we glimpse what threatens both stability and quest:

> As streams are, power is; those blessed flowers that dwell
> At the rough stream's calm head, thrive and prove well,
> But having left their roots, and themselves given
> To the stream's tyrannous rage, alas are driven
> Through mills, and rocks, and woods, and at last, almost
> Consumed in going, in the sea are lost.

Those lines remind us that the turbulence of Donne's world in the 1590s is not confined to developments in literature. They speak out of the harsh conflicts of religious and political allegiance in late sixteenth-century England; they bring into a fiercer focus that concern with the self and its integrity around which those early satires and verse-letters recurrently swoop.

Donne's Ovid: the Elegies

'The work of translation', said Eliot in a suggestive half-truth, 'is to make something foreign, or something remote in time, live with our own life' [1928, p.93]. This is what happens in the relation of some English poets of the 1590s to Ovid. Marlowe's brilliant corrugated translation of his love elegies, the *Amores*, was posthumously published in 1598. The Ovid of the *Metamorphoses* is a strong influence on Spenser and on the early Shakespeare as well as on the erotic epyllion, a mythological narrative poem in a wittily elegant style, of which *Venus and Adonis* and *Hero and Leander* are the leading examples. Translation is, literally, a carrying across. To take in both translation (as practised by Marlowe in relation to Ovid) and imitation (as practised by Donne) one might use the term *transplanting*, which carries suggestions of uprooting and of bedding down in a new soil. For translation and imitation alike involve a carrying across not only from one language and culture to another, but from a language and culture at a particular phase of its development. Hence in all such transfer there is bound to be loss for the resources of the two languages, the gifts of the two authors, can never be fully matched. Neither can the contexts out of which original and translation come. There is no English equivalent for Marlowe or Donne of the Augustan political order or of its celebration in Virgil's *Aeneid* against which Ovid's disclaiming of public themes in the *Amores* partly defines itself. In creative translation, however, there is a counterbalancing gain. Possibilities only latent in the original may be released; the receiving literature may be enriched by the entry and part-naturalising in it of what is foreign. This is what happens with Marlowe's translation of the *Amores*; what happens, much more unevenly, with Donne's imitation.

An elegy in modern usage is a poem of lament or meditation on death and loss; in Greek and Latin it is simply a poem written in the elegiac metre and the work of the three Roman elegists, Propertius, Ovid and Tibullus, is largely, though not exclusively, love poetry. In Ovid and Propertius it is a love poetry defined partly by its rejection of political themes and public affairs (e.g. *Amores* 1:1): a love poetry subjective, exclusive, even wilful. This, however, needs to be qualified in two ways. First, by turning their backs so explicitly on the public world the elegists ensure that that world shadows, if it does not define, the area in which they move.

Secondly, despite its subjectivity this is a love poetry pervaded by a sense of society and of social life; in Propertius and Ovid it is akin at times to the brilliant man-about-town poetry achieved in the early nineteenth century by Byron in English and in Russian by Pushkin. The affair or affairs that Ovid presents are played out in a world latticed with social and domestic detail. It is a world of siestas and dinner-parties, of street processions and an afternoon at the races; a world of clandestine messages sent by slaves, of doorkeepers and ladies' maids and an old bawd; of Corinna's planned sea voyage, from which Ovid tries to dissuade her, and of her buying a wig, about which he teases her.

Roman elegy offers, finally, a love poetry consciously elegant and wholly naturalistic. It is naturalistic in the sense that the love it presents, certainly in Ovid, is a this-worldly phenomenon, with no gleam of the religious or the transcendent upon it. It entirely lacks the adoration and humility that is central to (for example) much medieval love poetry. Its elegance is, correspondingly, carried into a poetry of love as seduction and game, deliberately outrageous and suave. Not that this is the whole of the *Amores*. They encompass a direct poetry of erotic encounter (as in 1:5, the starting-point for Donne's Elegy 19) and of a nerve-brushing sensuousness. They also encompass a poetry of loss (as in 3:8) and a poetry of darker passion (as in 3:14 where the instruction is no longer light-hearted but warped by a tormenting jealousy).

Donne's relation to Ovid in the *Elegies* allows us to see him, as nothing else in his *oeuvre* does, in relation to a single model. The involvement with another writer, the interaction of the given and the original which it sets up, projects features of his own sensibility as on a screen. Some of these features are among his least attractive. The zest for the grotesque can take a downturn into the nasty. The masterful energy readily degenerates into the swaggering or the brutal. The fragmentation that threatens the *Satires* is intensified. At their least creative the *Elegies* simply recycle an Ovidian motif (as Elegy 20 does with love-as-war) and, in trying to heighten, blunt; or, as in Elegy 1: 'Jealousy' or Elegy 7 they rehearse Ovidian positions with a hectoring energy which readily spills into mere overbearing. Even when he imitates creatively Donne's success can be uneven. Elegy 19: 'To his Mistress Going to Bed' which converts the erotic memory of *Amores* 1:5 into imperious address is one of those poems that wears less well with prolonged acquaintance: its joking comes to seem less exuberant than smug; the triumphant cry of its central lines ('O my America, my new found land') with their suggestive paradox ('To enter in these bonds, is to be free') retains all its power but cannot mesh with what surrounds it.

Some of these defects are intensified by the elegies' form. Or it might be more accurate to say that their couplet form allows the defects to emerge more sharply, especially when Donne writes in closed couplets, as in 'The Comparison' or in 'Love's War'. The effect is dogged or, at best, staccato. His couplet writing is at its happiest when his unit is not the individual couplet but the (flexibly graphed) verse-paragraph, seen at its best in the superb sweep and reversals of Elegy 16: 'On his Mistress'.

In the latter (which draws on *Amores* 2:11) the masculine voice is compelling, not overbearing, because its energy is now urgent with fear and love, fear not only for the woman addressed but for the speaker himself. In his potent final imagining of her dream, in which she sees him slain as he goes 'oe'er the white Alps alone', that fear is simultaneously evoked and, doubly, displaced: displaced into *her* dream (which *he* imagines) and evoked only in his forbidding her to dream it. The effect is persuasive and at the same time strange. It is persuasive in its releasing of deep natural fears, strange partly in the tension which *this* releasing of them creates. And that strangeness reaches back to meet and rechannel the sense of danger and of danger charged with mystery that presses on the poem from its opening lines.

'On his Mistress' is, I think, one of the two finest of the *Elegies*, the other being 'The Autumnal' in which Donne's imagination of the grotesque branches towards the temperate and, finally, towards the strange. It issues from his crossing of the forms of Ovidian elegy with those of the paradox. The paradox as a literary genre is popular in the Renaissance. Two forms widely practised are the mock-encomium or speech in praise of something obviously unpraiseworthy, trivial or vile, and the mock-argument in favour of a morally extravagant or indefensible position. Under the first we get such things as praises of baldness or lice; Nashe wrote an exuberant pamphlet in praise of red herring. The second is a natural device for displaying ingenuity and many of them are predictably tiresome though it can also be a vehicle for satire and even profundity as it is in one of the greatest Renaissance specimens of the genre, Erasmus' *Praise of Folly*. Both forms are found in Donne's prose *Paradoxes*, youthful work but often fetching and sometimes penetrating.

The same could not be said for some of the paradox-writing in the *Elegies*. Elegy 2: 'The Anagram' begins with a parody of the traditional blazon or feature-by-feature praise of a woman's beauty. It becomes more distinctively Donne in the finger-ticking pseudo-arguments of its central stretch which recall the prose *Paradoxes* but are aggressive in an ugly way that the latter are not. From this it half-lifts into a freer satirical praise of Flavia's ugliness to end with the couplet: 'One like none, and liked of none, fittest were,/ For, things in fashion every man will wear'. It is difficult to believe that the author of a poem as dismissively cheap as in the end this is – and it is not uncharacteristic of the worst elements in the *Elegies* – could also give us the desolate grandeur of the 'Nocturnal' or the masculine delicacy of a 'Valediction: forbidding Mourning', or, for that matter, a poem as haunting as 'The Autumnal'.

It is the most ingenious of the paradox-elegies but its ingenuities are bent to the praise of a tempered beauty of middle or old age. It is an unstable poem, lapsing readily into the grotesque as in the lines on the woman's wrinkles as Love's graves or on the 'winter-faces' 'Whose every tooth to a several place is gone,/ To vex their souls at Resurrection'. But the first of these is met by the dancing precision of the four lines that follow and the second is raised only to be rebuffed as the poem moves – one might almost say lurches – into the superb cadence, elegaic in our modern sense, of its closing lines:

> I hate extremes; yet I had rather stay
>> With tombs, than cradles, to wear out a day.
> Since such love's natural lation is, may still
>> My love descend, and journey down the hill,
> Not panting after growing beauties, so,
>> I shall ebb out with them, who homeward go.

Donne: the Songs and Sonnets

The *Songs and Sonnets* are simply the most *exhilarating* body of love poetry in English. That is what a rapid reading or re-reading of them prompts one to exclaim. They are exhilarating because of the range of moods and stances in love that they voice; because

of the intensity with which these are explored; and because of
the wit which aerates all. They give an anthology of topics and
motifs from two thousand years of European love poetry; at the
same time they largely master the problems of fragmentation,
brutality, overbearing that dog Donne in the *Satires* and *Elegies*.
Their range owes something to the meeting of radically different
traditions – Ovidian, Petrarchan, Neo-Platonic – in Renaissance
love-poetry (cf. the last studies cited for Donne in the section on
'Criticism since 1921' above); their energy and the variety of their
forms is Donne's own.

His invention of lyric forms is astonishing in its resourcefulness.
Their frequent intricacy combines freedom with discipline. One
impulse which powers the intricacy is suggested in 'The Triple
Fool': 'Grief brought to numbers cannot be so fierce,/ For, he
tames it, that fetters it in verse'(and note the interplay of this
with the sea image in the lines that precede). Characteristically,
such mastery is no sooner achieved than it is skewed: 'Some man,
his art and voice to show,/ Doth set and sing my pain,/ And, by
delighting many, frees again/ Grief, which verse did restrain'
(where 'my pain' may take in both the original suffering and
the strenuous art which seemed to have mastered it). The poem
illustrates both the irony Donne plays on his own situation and
the boundaries of such irony in the irritable prose precision of
the final line: 'Who are a little wise, the best fools be'. ('The
Triple Fool' also opens up perspectives on Donne's straddle
between public and private, his position as a poet writing for
circulation in manuscript rather than for print.)

The valuing of intricacy here might be contrasted with that
in a sermon passage where Donne says of the Psalms that their
form is 'both curious, and requires diligence in the making, and
when it is made, can have nothing, no syllable taken from it, or
added to it'. This suggests the other appeal of intricate form for
Donne: its elegance (it is 'curious' in the Renaissance sense of
finely wrought) and the completeness it possesses. It is in his lyrics,
with their combination of discipline and freedom, that he achieves
that completeness as he rarely does in his non-lyric verse.

The achievement of the lyrics can be grasped if we compare
those that handle Ovidian motifs with the bulk of the elegies.
The rake's swagger of the latter becomes a blithe and singing
impudence in 'The Indifferent' (which catches one Ovidian tone
better than anything in the *Elegies*); their argumentation becomes

acrobatic in 'The Flea'. The group of poems addressed to the God of Love picks out darker elements of exasperation and pursuit. But the range, even within this group, is worth noting: how exasperation turns both self-mocking and celebratory in 'Love's Exchange'; how it achieves a lucid sweep in 'Love's Deity'; how 'Love's Diet' gives the Ovidian pursuit a brutal assertiveness but wins from its stanza form a flexibility that enables Donne to carry off the brutality with a certain dash he cannot compass in the *Elegies*. And finally one can cite 'Love's Growth' to illustrate how the rejection of religious or transcendent claims ('Love's not so pure, and abstract, as they use/ To say, which have no mistress but their muse') is only the prelude to a celebration in which human love is – not absorbed but – opened into the rhythms of nature which in the end it rides.

The freedom of Donne's lyrics is at its most obvious in quasi-conversational pieces like 'Woman's Constancy' or 'The Apparition' which build up through one prolonged unit, weaving sequences of rhyme across different line-lengths to create an un-resting movement and a final crescendo. But how distinctive the effects are: 'Woman's Constancy' winding through an almost blasé catalogue to a climax of casual insult, 'The Apparition' snakingly intense. The combination of freedom with discipline is seen at its most strenuous in poems like 'The Curse' or 'The Expiration' which mount their rhetorical assault through a cross-weaving of syntax or sound effects. They develop the boxing-in effects we have seen Donne secure through syntax in the couplet poems, making them at once more supple and more intense. Akin to them but more shifting and angular are the refrain poems like 'The Will', 'Love's Deity', 'The Prohibition'. The common effect of refrains is to act as a stabilising keel to their poems. They evoke a sense of the fixed, at their most potent a sense of the unchanging, of that which transcends the immediate action or mood of the poem. Hence they often have a quality of the proverbial or the liturgical, a quality at once resonant and opaque. This is the quality we find in a ballad like 'Green Grow the Rushes O!' or in the clangorous refrain of Dunbar's resurrection hymn *Surrexit Dominus de sepulchro* or in Villon's haunting *Mais ou sont les neiges d'antan?* Donne eschews such effects in favour of riddling and twisting refrains. This costs him the impersonal power that Dunbar or Villon can command. It gives instead the satisfaction of having discrete detail or riddling assertion suddenly, ingeniously, locked into pattern.

These boxing-in effects come to their climax in Donne's miniaturising and in the stanza forms that reinforce it in poems like 'The Good Morrow', 'The Sun Rising', 'The Anniversary' and perhaps 'The Canonization'. In the first three of these Donne deploys superbly what might be called a telescoping stanza form.

I call it telescoping because each of them builds up a syntactic and rhyming unit in the first half of the stanza from which it launches out in the second half through a lengthening series of lines, usually rhyming on a single sound:

> And now good morrow to our waking souls,
>   Which watch not one another out of fear;
> For love, all love of other sights controls,
>   And makes one little room an every where.
> Let sea-discoverers to new worlds have gone,
> Let maps to others, worlds on worlds have shown,
> Let us possess one world, each hath one and is one.
>
> ['The Good Morrow']

The last three lines create a sense of mounting and widening sweep as rhythm and syntax accelerate – to swoop down into the pulsing repose of the final alexandrine.

Very different is the effect of quatrain poems like 'A Valediction: forbidding Mourning' and (at least some of the time) 'The Ecstasy'. In these Donne calls out the potential of the basic stanza form for spaced and balanced statement. He does so through a measured, sometimes pausing, rhythm and through a diction that seems (and this from the author of some of the *Satires* and *Elegies!*) effortlessly pellucid and grave. It is a style too aristocratic to call attention to itself; but it can achieve effects of unobtrusive precision whether mimetic (as in 'The Ecstasy', 'Because such fingers need to knit/ That subtle knot, which makes us man') or aching (as in the 'Valediction', 'Care less eyes, lips and hands to miss). And its lucidity can charge the single unexpected word with a commanding richness as in the central stanza of 'The Ecstasy':

> When love, with one another so
>   Interinanimates two souls,
> That abler soul, which thence doth flow,
>   Defects of loneliness controls

where the richness is in the verbs 'interinanimates' and 'flow'
and in the interplay between them (and also between them and
that moving final line).

It is characteristic of Donne's lyrics (as against the more
verbally aggressive *Elegies* and *Satires*) to charge a single word or
phrase in this unpredictable way. One might contrast the dislo-
cation effect of the famous line in Elegy 4, 'Even my oppressed
shoes, dumb and speechless were' in its – very different - verbal
context. The effect depends partly on the prose exactness that
the *Songs and Sonnets* readily command whether the exactness be
matter-of-fact (as in 'The Dissolution' or 'Love's Infiniteness') or
singing (as in 'Break of Day'). To one side of this charging lie
more assertive effects like those of 'The Apparition' ('And then
poor aspen wretch, neglected thou/ Bathed in a cold quicksilver
sweat wilt lie') or the 'melted maid' and the 'ragged bony name'
which will be 'my ruinous anatomy' in 'A Valediction: of my
Name in the Window' or the 'naked thinking heart' in 'The
Blossom' which springs out of the coiling argument the poem so
effortlessly sustains. And one might contrast *that* effect with the
beautifully unobtrusive use of 'nestle' in the second stanza of the
same poem.

To the other side lie those effects – which I find among the
most potent in Donne – when a pellucid image or line suddenly
swims free, often from an overwrought or uneasy poem. We have
seen this happen with 'The Autumnal'. It happens at the end of
the funeral elegy for Prince Henry (which Ben Jonson reported
Donne as saying he had written to match the elegy by Herbert's
brother, Sir Edward, in obscurity) with its final line: 'I were an
angel, singing what you were'. In the *Songs and Sonnets* it happens
in 'The Relic'; and it is with it and 'Twickenham Garden' I
shall end.

The former is a splendid set-piece that uses the Petrarchan
conventions not to mock but to transpose the Petrarchan style
into an idiom that is distinctively Donne's. The anguish of the
Petrarchan lover becomes corrosive (as in the final lines). The
Petrarchan plangency becomes a vehement interplay between the
speaker and the natural world in the second stanza; and, above
all, metamorphosis which can be so potent in Petrarch (see e.g.
the twenty-third poem of his *Rime*) and which, certainly in the
Petrarchan or Ovidian forms, is so rare in Donne is here given
a full weight and edge, both in the second stanza and in that

great line of the first: 'the spider love, which transubstantiates all' – a line that could serve as a touchstone for one side of Donne's art.

'The Relic', by contrast, is a much more fragile and uncertain poem. Like its companion piece 'The Funeral' its tone is hard to pin down. It brings together a number of attitudes but one is puzzled to know how they combine or whether they are simply jumbled together. How does the sardonic parenthesis ('For graves have learned that woman-head/ To be to more than one a bed') fit with the famous 'bracelet of bright hair about the bone' that almost immediately follows? How does one read the dramatising (mock-dramatising?), with its tinge of blasphemy, of the digging-up scene Donne envisages? And what does one make of the final stanza which evokes Ovidian naturalism ('Our hands ne'er touched the seals,/ Which nature, injured by late law, sets free') – but evokes it in the context of an innocence extravagantly childish? And yet it is out of this that Donne steps with one of the most convincing of his assertions of the transcendence of the love he records – or so at least I find it, though I can see why some readers consider it flat:

> These miracles we did; but now alas,
> All measure, and all language, I should pass,
> Should I tell what a miracle she was.

Donne: the religious poetry

Though not large in bulk Donne's religious poetry is notably varied – in quality and in forms. In the latter there is continuity with the secular poetry and also new development. Couplet pieces like 'The Cross' or 'Good Friday, 1613' recall the Elegies in their handling of that form, whether paragraphed or staccato. 'A Hymn to God the Father' with its refrain, still more its interlocking structure, recalls poems like 'The Will' or 'The Curse'. The 'Hymn to Christ' has a seven-line stanza divided 4/3 like 'The Good Morrow' but uses it to probe and wrestle rather than exultantly to celebrate. On the other side the sonnet – a form marginal in the earlier poetry – becomes central and is yoked with extra-literary forms of prayer: the public prayer of liturgy in 'La Corona' the dramatising, inner prayer and analysis of the meditation in the *Holy Sonnets*; and in the most extended and ambitiously experimental of the religious poems, *A Litany*, Donne tries to bend an impersonal form of public confession and appeal to purposes of witty exploration.

The variable quality of the religious poetry also needs stressing. Too often it is treated – especially in the *Holy Sonnets* which can be taken as its core – as if it were all of a piece. Yet surely one of the first things to strike a reader is how decidedly the latter vary in procedure and in success.

The least successful are those like Sonnet 15 whose opening lines ('Wilt thou love God, as he thee? Then digest/ My soul, this wholesome meditation') say all that needs to be said about it: it is a set meditation to be worked through and nothing has been done to energise this into a poem. At the opposite extreme come sonnets like 4 ('O my black soul') and 6 ('This is my play's last scene') which create a pivotal drama of salvation. It is pivotal because the octave evokes the plight of the sin-stricken soul, galvanised by sickness, death and the prospect of judgement; the sestet offers the salvation which will answer that plight. Such a drama is congenial to some of the deepest drives in Donne's sensibility. It satisfies his extremism and his fascination with the interlocking of opposites. And there is no doubting the power with which the drama is created. He has seized on the possibilities of the Petrarchan sonnet form with the enclosing structures its rhyme scheme affords and the opportunities implicit in its octave/sestet division for massing and confrontation. He has harnessed this to the drama inherent in the meditation as a form of prayer and by pitting octave against sestet, terror against redemption, created poems at once comprehensive and intense.

Or would have, had those sonnets realised the possibilities one can see them shadowing forth. The trouble is that the dramatising of terror outweighs the salvation that should swallow it up. The latter seems either contrived – a kind of theological tiddleywinks ('wash thee in Christ's blood, which has this might/ That being red, it dyes red souls to white') or else limp. And this failure ruins the pivotal effects they attempt. More than that, it makes the dramatising of sin and terror in the octave suspect: if it can be so easily swept away does it not smack of the contrived?

The *Holy Sonnets* I find wear best on continued reading are those in which Donne accepts his fluctuating devotion, the incongruities of his spiritual life, without trying for a dramatic resolution. Only, 'accepts' is too serene for pieces as troubled as 19 ('Oh, to vex me, contraries meet in one'), as sombre as 3 ('O might those sighs and tears return again'). These read like diary extracts, pieces of self-analysis that get no further. The finest of them is 'Thou hast made me, and shall thy work decay?' which moulds the experience of instability towards the beautiful interplay of its close where the flutter of hope in the penultimate line is overborne by the assurance of the last: 'Thy grace may wing me to prevent his art/ And thou like adamant draw mine iron heart'.

Even if one finds the *Holy Sonnets* badly uneven as a group one has to admit the variety of directions in which they jet. It is for that reason I claimed them as the core – core not climax – of Donne's religious poetry. Much of what they endeavour he carries further in the freer movements or more elaborated forms of *A Litany* and the *Hymns*. One danger for the more dramatic sonnets is that their intense confined drama of confrontation with God will end either in crowding out any sense of his presence or at least in cutting short any sense of a developing relationship with him. Their speaker's encounter with God takes place, so to speak, under a bell-jar. Such a narrowing concentration is precisely what the 'Hymn to God the Father' undertakes and drives further than any of the *Holy Sonnets*, creating echo-chamber effects with its repetitions and blockings, summed up in the famous refrain. But in the refrain itself there is a conscious irony [Sanders, 1972, p.144] and at its climax the poem transforms its own key stylistic feature, the repetitions and counterings that create the sense of the self trapped in its sins and fears, 'that sin, through which I run,/ And do run still: though still I do deplore'. These counterings are now funnelled into the appeal to God: 'Swear by thy self'; the headlong movement up to this point is slowed in the monosyllabic half-line 'that at my death thy son' as the poem gathers itself into a wave-poise before crashing down in its final blend of exhaustion and triumph: 'And, having done that, thou hast done/ I fear no more'. (The manuscript reading of 'have' for 'fear' in the last line would intensify this blending of opposed emotions.)

Seen in this way as the triumphant terminus of one group of the *Holy Sonnets* the 'Hymn to God the Father' stands aside from

the other two Hymns and *A Litany* which I consider the peaks of
Donne's religious poetry. *A Litany* explores with a quirky fullness
and rigour the complex life of the believer in an ambiguous world.
The ambiguity is partly that experienced by the Christian who
is also (in a rich and not simply perjorative sense of the term) a
worldly man – a man versed in the ways of the world and subject
to their corruptions but recognising their valid appeal. Donne,
the aspiring civil servant who had wrecked a brilliant career by
a reckless love-marriage and who spent the bleak middle years
of his life (out of which *A Litany* comes) angling for positions and
engaging in journey-work, was such a man. The strength of the
poem is not in its elaborate invoking of God and the saints but
in the energy with which it weaves between extremes (e.g. sts
XV–XVIII). The moderation for which it strives is searchingly
resilient and self-aware and at its climax moderation passes into
something else in the magnificent cry: 'That our affections kill
us not, nor die,/ Hear us, weak echoes, O thou ear, and cry'.

A Litany and the 'Hymn to Christ' offer a classic religious poetry
of middle age (Eliot's *Four Quartets* come to mind as an analogue
on this score). The hymn is a poem of loss and renunciation as
the 'Hymn to God, my God' is a poem of loss and celebration.
The first life of Donne claims that the latter was written on his
death-bed but this is disputed. It is in any case a poem written in
the expectation of death and it brings to a climax issues that run
through all his work. The most fundamental of these is the
masterfulness that stamps it from the *Satires* on. It is a masterfulness in sporadic interplay throughout Donne's career with a
desire to be mastered and overcome. The latter is predictably
strengthened in some of the religious poetry and can take un-
pleasant forms as in 'Batter my heart'. The interplay is at
its strongest in some of his meditations on death and resurrection. In a revealing passage of a letter to his friend Goodyear
he says that he wishes death to 'win me and overcome me . . .
when I must shipwrack, I would do it in a Sea . . . not in a
sullen weedy lake, where I could not have so much as exercise
for my swimming'.

The imagery of the sea and voyaging which always releases
some of Donne's deepest imaginative energies comes magnificently to the fore in all three hymns. In this one it fuses a
sense of profound passivity with adventuring alertness: 'this is
my south-west discovery/ *Per fretum febris*, by these straits to die'.

It recalls, as neither of the other two hymns does, the imagery and sweep of poems like 'The Good Morrow' with their miniaturising and opening out as, in a different way, it recalls the end of 'The Autumnal'; and the self-dramatising of his earlier poetry finds its consummation in the gathering up of his death-bed drama into the cosmic drama of the dying and resurrected Christ:

> So, in his purple wrapped receive me Lord,
>> By these his thorns give me his other crown;
> And as to others' souls I preached thy word,
>> Be this my text, my sermon to mine own,
> Therefore that he may raise the Lord throws down.

Herbert and the Religious Poets

> Holiness is silence.
>> [Mauriac]

> It is the sweetest note that man can sing,
> When grace in vertues key tunes natures string.
>> [Southwell]

> SOUL: Seek out reality, leave things that seem.
> HEART: What, be a singer born and lack a theme?
> SOUL: Isaiah's coal, what more could man desire?
> HEART: Struck dumb in the simplicity of fire!
> SOUL: Look on that fire; salvation walks within.
> HEART: What theme had Homer but original sin?
>> [Yeats]

Herbert: problems of sacred poetry

The 'Jordan' poems are often taken as a point of entry for *The Temple* and, if so taken, they mislead. They are read as Herbert's manifesto: poems of dedication and rejection, setting out the purification verse must undergo in the service of God. But the purification they demand is so extreme it leaves them kamikaze pieces, no adequate guide to the complexity of his actual practice.

Their title calls up the passage of the Old Testament Israelites into the Promised Land and the baptism Christianity has traditionally seen that passage as prefiguring. It perhaps also (and more ominously) calls up the story of Naaman, the haughty pagan leper who finally submits to what seems the petty ritual of washing in the Jordan after which 'his flesh came again like unto the flesh of a little child' [2 Kings 5:9–15]. (This echo would be ominous because the simplicity of a child is not easily won – may even be ambiguous – in the case of a poet as self-conscious and sophisticated as Herbert.)

Both poems are preoccupied with questions of *style*: 'Jordan' (I) with a range of contemporary styles which it mockingly characterises and rejects, 'Jordan' (II) with the style of Herbert's own first attempts at religious poetry which he rejects no less caustically. But 'Jordan' (II) does not only reject; it analyses the dangers that beset Herbert as dedicated poet and its analysis is suggestive as well as surgically deft. There are the dangers of a chaotic fertility, of overelaboration, of a craftsmanship fussy in its straining at perfection. Double meanings insinuate themselves quietly ('excell', 'sought out quaint words'), with a touch of self-parody ('My thoughts began to burnish, sprout and swell'), and ostentation ('Decking the sense, as if it were to sell'). At the poem's climax doubleness reveals itself as duplicity: 'As flames do work and winde, when they ascend,/ So did I weave my self into the sense'. The restless revisings of the poet-craftsman are fired by religious devotion ('Nothing could seem too rich to clothe the sunne') and yet as he is released into the process of poetic creation the release itself declares a subtle egoism inherent – it would seem – in that process: 'So did I weave *my self* into the sense'. And once this has been exposed the labour and energy of fashioning that have gone before can be dismissed as 'bustle' and 'pretence' to which the answer is

> There is in love a sweetnesse readie penn'd;
> Copie out onely that, and save expense.

This is almost certainly not the simplistic declaration – love is enough – it may seem. The love is that of Christ and its copying may stretch to take in the whole life of the speaker as poet, priest and believer. This one could grant and still urge that 'copying' either leaves us in the dark as to what it involves or else implies a view of religious poetry that is more than questionably colourless and easy – not to mention that it would stifle some of Herbert's distinctive gifts.

The stance he elects at the end of 'Jordan' (I) – 'Who plainly say, *My God, My King* – is no less problematic. It gives us very little idea of what the poetry he wants might be like. It will presumably be a poetry of direct statement that confesses and adores. And one might say that all Christian adoration and confession are implicit in that bare ejaculation '*My God, My King*' as all Christian petition is enclosed in the prayer of Gethsemane: '*Thy will be done*'. yet, even if '*My God, My King*' marks both the starting point of worship and the climax at which it passes, in broken cry, beyond speech it is precisely between that starting point and that climax that religious poetry, as a fashioned utterance, must occur.

But if extreme the 'Jordan' poems are not eccentric. (Nor is their extremism uncharacteristic of Herbert. On the contrary, it is congenial to him on several fronts. It is congenial to the adolescent idealist who wrote to his mother, enclosing two ascetic sonnets, of his resolution 'that my poor Abilities in Poetry, shall be all, and ever consecrated to God's glory'. It is congenial to the courtier–intellectual into whose sensibility the rigorous Augustinian doctrines of grace have bitten deep. And it is congenial to the subtle, passionate, worldly aristocrat who wrote 'The Pearl' and who 'after much delay/ Much wrastling' renounced the prospect of a court career to become the rector of a small country parish.)

They are not eccentric because the questions they raise are fundamental. 'Jordan' (II) asks whether there may not be an egoism inherent in the activity of poetic creation that thwarts all attempts to dedicate it to God. Beyond that looms the question whether such egoism does not haunt and corrupt all attempts at dedication and sacrifice. It is a question with which Herbert will wrestle throughout *The Temple*. The simplicity of style both poems demand can be traced back to the roots of the Christian tradition: to the parables of Jesus as recorded in the first three gospels, to the distinctive style of the fourth with its combined lucidity and mystery, to the starkness of the Passion narratives and to the reticences of the Resurrection stories that are their elusive sequel.

'When a poet chooses a style, or chooses *between* styles', writes Donald Davie,

> he is making a choice in which his whole self is involved –
> including, if he is a Christian poet, that part of himself which

is most earnestly and devoutly Christian. The question is, for him: what sort of language is most appropriate when I would speak of, or to, my God? And it is not only the puritans among the poets who appear to have decided that the only language proper for such purposes is a language stripped of fripperies and seductive indulgences . . .when speaking to God, in poetry as in prayer, any sort of prevarication or ambiguity is unseemly, indeed unthinkable. [1981, pp.xxviii–ix]

That is challenging and obviously bears on Herbert's practice. Yet both the critic's claim and the poet's practice themselves need to be challenged. Davie loads the issues by making the choice one between 'fripperies and seductive indulgences' and 'the most direct and unswerving English'. But might a religious poetry not eschew the former while using language in ways that were not always 'direct and unswerving'? Might it not even find itself impelled to use language in such ways? Davie claims that the nature of worship both communal and personal demands simplicity: and again one can take the force of the claim but recall much religious poetry (Dante, Milton, the Song of Deborah, Smart) that is high-wrought without falling into seductive indulgences. (That said, one should also acknowledge how readily the high-wrought falls into just such indulgences: some medieval hymns or, in our present field, Crashaw, might provide notable examples.)

And as for simplicity, even as a goal, may it not prove to be less simple than the 'Jordan' poems would have it? We might put the question by quoting the judgement with which Eliot seals an early review: 'Great simplicity is only won by an intense moment or by years of intelligent effort, or by both. It represents one of the most arduous conquests of the human spirit: the triumph of feeling and thought over the natural sin of language' [1919].

Herbert: contexts for sacred poetry

Herbert is exceptional in the rigour with which he pursues the questions raised by a dedicated and exclusive religious poetry. But in writing such a poetry he participates in an aspiration and programme recurrently voiced through the English Renaissance and first realised in the 1590s by the Jesuit poet and martyr, Robert Southwell. The immediate context for this programme in the later sixteenth century is the break-up of Christendom, the political and cultural order of the Middle Ages under the twin impact of the Renaissance and the Reformation. It would be absurd to claim the medieval order as unequivocally Christian, still more to claim it as harmoniously integrated by its Christianity. Ages of faith are, almost by definition, also ages of heresy and medieval Christendom is often riven by conflict. Nonetheless the existence of an order in which politics, culture and society are walled round and interpenetrated by Christianity does give its religious poets a certain unself-conscious stability and calm not possible to those of our period. The dangers for the latter are, on the one hand, overassertiveness, on the other the withdrawal into a world-rejecting piety that rapidly becomes cosy or stuffy. This in turn brings up the question whether there is not something *inherently* limited in a dedicated religious poetry. It is the question voiced with laconic magnificence by Yeats in the lines at the head of this section that finally reject the religious stance they have considered: 'What theme had Homer but original sin?' It is the question voiced more circumspectly by Eliot when he concedes some validity to the view that the religious poet 'is leaving out what men consider their major passions, and thereby confessing his ignorance of them' [Eliot, 1951, p.390].

Against those dangers can be set the resources that their new situation offers the religious poets of Herbert's time. Reformation and Counter-Reformation have brought about massive developments in theology, in devotional life and, not least, in Bible translation and liturgy. Active in an early seventeenth-century milieu are the radical insights of the Protestant Reformation, the massive theology, bracing or daunting, of Calvin, the analyses of the spiritual life by the Spanish masters, Ignatius, Teresa, John of the Cross – not to mention, nearer home, the English Bible and the Book of Common Prayer. Not to mention either the continued presence of much in medieval and earlier Christianity and its interaction with the new developments. What any poet makes of these resources is another matter and obviously no poet will be open equally to them all. But the matrix they provide is enormously fertile and its fertility is increased by the continual activity of translation, adaptation and controversy that goes on across the denominational divides.

A more specific context is provided by the Protestant emphasis on the Book of Psalms as mirroring the experience of the Christian believer. The Anglican liturgy which Herbert would have followed as priest of Bemerton prescribed the reading through of the entire Psalter once a month in the course of Mattens and Evensong. It provides the key *model* for *The Temple* as the sonnet-sequences (which C.S. Lewis has described as offering an erotic liturgy) provide its key secular *analogue*.

Both Psalter and sonnet-sequences present a body of lyric neither rigidly ordered nor random. They repeat and vary key motifs and at the same time allow for the intense local development of individual (and contrasting or contradictory) moods. They offer indefinite possibilities of echo and cross-reference; the build-up of fluid local groupings and the development of perspectives which can shift dramatically or can open up a single commanding view. Of the English Renaissance sequences Sidney's *Astrophel and Stella* is the most dramatic, Shakespeare's the most suggestive in its fluidity. Herbert in *The Temple* carries such fluidity to the point of virtuosity. There are poems emphatically juxtaposed like 'The Crosse' and 'The Flower'. There are poems which *may* interact across a distance like those titled 'Affliction'. Or a sequence, like that from 'Antiphon' (I) to 'Praise' (I), may suggest groupings that shift and reform as one reads them in series, creating as they do so different centre-points and different perspectives.

Bringing Psalter and sonnet-sequences together like this reminds us that *The Temple* also has its secular contexts. 'The Pearl' displays with a flexible magnificence how intimately Herbert knows the worlds of Renaissance learning and the Renaissance court that he has renounced – and with what an aching exactness he can write: 'I know the ways of pleasure, the sweet strains,/ The lullings and the relishes of it'! (It is the same temperament that gives us the sensuous finesse of 'The Flower': 'And now in age I bud again./ After so many deaths I live and write;/ I once more smell the dew and rain/ And relish versing'.) And he can explicitly rechannel as well as recall, as he does for instance with secular love poetry in the paired sonnets 'Love' (I) and (II). Such rechannelling is, indeed, one principal way in which he can pursue his vocation as an exclusive religious poet while circumventing the dangers of narrowness that attend on it.

The last context I want to propose is that supplied by the biblical usages of 'temple' from which Herbert's volume takes its name. The New Testament inherits the concept with a complex load of history and memories from the Old. It uses it metaphorically to articulate the shift from physical building and public worship to the worship offered in the lives of believers. But this shift is by no means simply an inward or spiritualising movement. For the temple metaphor is also used to articulate the relation of believers to Christ who had spoken of his own body as the temple [John 2:13–22]. In some key passages [e.g. Ephesians 2:20–22 and First Peter 2:1–11] metaphors of building are crossed with those of growth and the reference to Christ as 'the chief corner stone in whom the whole building fitly framed together groweth unto an holy temple in the Lord' [Ephesians 2:20–1] carries us beyond metaphor altogether. Such New Testament passages seem to bring together different kinds of language – the historical, the metaphorical, the metaphysical – in ways that are suggestive and baffling in the highest degree. But we can at least claim that they present Herbert with a controlling metaphor that is not only fluid and complex but mysterious in ways that may have something to do with the strangeness that finally marks *The Temple* for all the simplicity towards which it strives. (We might also notice that there is one emphasis in the New Testament use of the temple-complex which Herbert significantly does not take up and that is the emphasis on the breaking or displacement of the temple which reaches from the ministry of Jesus to the final apocalyptic vision of the New Jerusalem in which there is no temple: 'for the Lord God Almighty and the Lamb are the temple of it' [Revs 21:22].)

Herbert and vocation

Herbert is not only a dedicated religious poet, he probes the nature and cost of that dedication with a resourcefulness unsurpassed in English. Individual poems explore his vocation as preacher ('The Windows'); as priest ('Aaron'); as testator ('Obedience'); as servant, whether protesting (e.g. 'Affliction' I) or lamenting his unfruitfulness (e.g. 'Employment' I) or rebellious (e.g. 'The Collar') until his rebellion is dispersed by the divine voice which calls to him not as a servant but as a child; as God's musician ('Easter') and as his music (e.g. 'The Temper' I). The sequence of poems from 'The Altar' to 'Easter-Wings' and later pieces like 'The Holdfast' face the problems raised by the strict Augustinian doctrines of grace which insist not only that all human service of God is a response to a prior divine action but that even response itself is only made possible by grace.

The first poem of *The Temple* proper enacts the rearing of an altar but it is a broken altar 'made of a heart, and cemented with teares' whose 'parts are as thy hand did frame;/ No workman's tool hath touched the same'. And it closes with the double appeal: 'O let thy blessed SACRIFICE be mine,/ And sanctifie this ALTAR to be thine'. These lines set up at the very beginning of *The Temple* a *transposition* of the divine and the human which is one of the fundamental patterns of Herbert's imagination. I discuss below some ways in which that transposition is worked out. In the present sequence the closing lines of 'The Altar' also open it to *The Sacrifice* which follows. It is a monologue spoken by Christ from the cross which deploys the Christian paradoxes of redemption with a hammering energy of rhythm and irony. It is a poem relentlessly objective to a degree that shuts out any human response, in one sense shuts out any human presence at all. Response is what Herbert attempts in the next poem, 'The Thanksgiving', only for it to be gradually revealed as a rivalry with God, a turning back of his art of love upon him, which is both presumptuous and impossible: 'Then for thy passion – I will do for that –/ Alas, my God, I know not what.' This is the egoism lurking in what seems dedication that 'Jordan' (II), less exuberantly, lays bare. But instead of falling back on the direct-ness of 'Jordan' (II)'s 'copying' this sequence pursues a complex interplay of divine action and human response. In its third poem 'Reprisall' (titled in an earlier version 'The Second Thanks-giving') the sober recognition that 'there is no dealing with thy mighty passion' is met by the yearning of 'O make me innocent that I/ May give a disentangled state and free' and both steady into the final acknowledgment: 'Though I can do nought/ Against thee, in thee I will overcome/ The man, who once against thee fought'. The style of 'The Reprisall' is deliberately prosaic and exact but within that exactness it distils a chastened lyricism that beautifully renders the relation with God that Herbert finally attains. The lyricism of 'Easter', the other climax of this sequence, is, by con-trast, song-like and soaring. But it too is only attained through the struggle first to respond to what God has done and finally to integrate that response *within* what he continues to do: 'since all musick is but three parts vied/ And multiplied,/ O let thy blessed Spirit bear a part,/ And make up our defects with his sweet art'.

This invoking of God to enter and complete the praise which a poem offers him is one of Herbert's key strategies in *The Temple* and one of the outworkings of what I have called the pattern of transposition. In such transposition the human opens itself to the divine, the divine encloses and transforms the human. At its most thoroughgoing it is formulated in the third definition of prayer offered in the first sonnet of that title: 'God's breath in man returning to his birth'. This combines echoes of the creation story in Genesis 2, where God breathes the breath of life into man's nostrils, with the Pauline teaching [Romans 8:23–7] that in the struggle and yearning, sometimes broken or inarticulate, of prayer God in the Spirit speaks, through man, to himself. To one side of such transposition lies the trim equipoise of divine and human expressed in a later line from the same sonnet: 'heaven in ordinarie, man well drest'. To the other lie those moments of an ultimate accord between God and man in which all struggle for adequate response, all fretting at human sin and human limitation, are transcended.

Such an accord is one of the final homing-places of Herbert's imagination. It can equally be lyrical,

> Whether I flie with angels, fall with dust,
> Thy hands made both, and I am there:
> Thy power and love, my love and trust
> Make one place ev'ry where
>
> [The Temper' (I)]

or matter-of-fact,

> You must sit down, sayes Love, and taste my meat:
> So I did sit and eat.
>
> ['Love' (III)]

If an ultimate homing-place, those accords are also hard-won and not to be sustained. 'Temper' (II) opens: 'It cannot be. Where is that mightie joy/ Which just now took up all my heart?' Herbert's living through of his vocation makes him a poet both of religious conflict and of mundane experience, of life as it is lived daily and hourly, with its fluctuating inner weather of mood and response. He can bring out the bleakness (or the frightening intensities) of such mundane experience as acutely as Cowper or

Larkin: the frustrations of sickness and thwarted plans ('Affliction' I), the experience of hope deferred (e.g. 'Home') and prayer unanswered (e.g. 'Deniall') and mental turmoil ('My thoughts are all a case of knives,/ Wounding my heart/ With scattered smart,/ As watering pots give flowers their lives') ('Affliction' IV); the sense of his own life as sterile (e.g. 'Grace') which deepens into the fear of oncoming age and decaying powers in 'The Forerunners'.

It is out of such experiences that his acutest conflicts come. They are not the conflicts over personal salvation that rack Bunyan and some of his characters, or the conflicts of faith and doubt familiar in much nineteenth-century and modern poetry. They are not even – directly – the familiar struggle between the claims of God and those of the world. Herbert writes in *The Temple* from the position of one who has already made his renunciations. His sufferings come from the pang of memory as he recalls the fuller life he has renounced or frets at his present confinement. But they come most acutely when he has to confront the fact that after he has renounced so much to serve God, God seems not to want his service. What it means to have a vocation and then to find it thwarted by God is set out in 'The Crosse' with a terrible stony precision – 'To have my aim, and yet to be/ Farther from it then when I bent my bow;/ To make my hopes my torture, and the fee/Of all my woes another wo' – that climaxes in the cry 'these contrarieties crush me: these crosse actions/ Do winde a rope about, and cut my heart'. From the entrapment defined by those puns and the final homely image Herbert can only escape in a transposition made laconic by extremity as he projects his suffering into the life of God by making his own Christ's prayer in the face of his Passion: '*Thy will be done.*'

Herbert and the homely

I spoke earlier of the rooting of simplicity, for Christian writers, in the gospels. Such a use of the homely and familiar to image the kingdom of God is held, for Christian belief, within the fundamental mystery of the Incarnation. To believe that, in the key-text of the Fourth Gospel, 'the Word became flesh', that the nature of God and his relations with man are definitively revealed in the life and death of a first-century Jewish carpenter turned freelance rabbi, is to hold that the infinite is revealed in

the finite, the divine in the everyday and the ultimate in what
is homely, even trivial. Conceptually it generates paradoxes like
the *Verbum Infans*, 'the Word unable to speak a word' that Eliot
in 'Gerontion' plucked from a sermon by Herbert's older friend
Lancelot Andrewes. Stylistically it leads to new ways of repre-
senting reality. The German scholar Auerbach in his classic study
of such representation in European literature, *Mimesis*, and in a
later essay on 'Sermo Humilis' [1957] has traced the emergence,
under the impact of Christianity, of a new style in which the most
exalted or serious subject-matter can be expressed in terms of the
everyday. *Sermo humilis* would be literally translated 'low style' but
it has built into its foundations an element of tension and paradox.
In the hands of such Christian masters of rhetoric as Saint Jerome
this element becomes flamboyant, the style acquires a dynamic
instability of great power. This separates it decisively from the
plain style defined by Winters as characterising some Renaissance
English poets. In Herbert we have a plain-style poet – or, rather,
one who drives the plain style towards the bare or the minimal
– but also a poet in whom the tempered precisions of the plain
style are open to being skewed by the extravagance of the *sermo
humilis*.

An extravagance, however, that is masked by the miniaturising
which Herbert carries further than any other of the Metaphysicals.
Donne addressing the Virgin writes:

> Thou'hast light in dark; and shutt'st in little room,
> *Immensity cloistered in thy dear womb.*
>
> ['La Carona'(II)]

The chorus of Crashaw's Nativity Hymn proclaims

> *Wellcome, all* WONDERS in one sight!
> AEternity shutt in a span.
> Sommer in Winter. Day in Night.
> Heaven in earth, and GOD in MAN.

Donne's lines have a spaced-out lucidity and a caressing intimacy
(note the play of 'little room' against 'Immensity' at the beginning
of the next line and the beautifully managed transition through
'cloistered' to 'thy dear womb'); Crashaw's have a dancing rapture
of cosmic celebration. Herbert is perceptibly, though modestly,
different from either;

O Thou, whose glorious, yet contractèd light,
Wrapt in nights mantle, stole into a manger . . .
['Christmas']

The extremism of miniaturising and of the homely in Herbert
can produce those effects of strangeness on which I want to end.
But more direct uses of both should be considered first.

Some modern studies of the gospel parables have rightly
urged that their simplicity can house the enigmatic and ironical,
can disrupt or dislocate expectation. Herbert's own view of them
in his prose treatise *A Priest to the Temple* [c.xxiii] is disappointingly
reductive, seeing them principally as teaching aids for more limited intelligences. In the poetry there are cases – 'Life' might be a
fair specimen – where homely detail functions, straightforwardly,
to illustrate. And there are more cases than one might wish like
'Jesu' or 'Love-joy' where miniaturising produces poems that are
cosy or, at best, over-ingeniously neat.

This cramping domestication of the divine is at its most disappointing in a poem like 'Providence'; at its most disappointing
because it is so ambitious a poem and because this kind of ranging
cosmic poetry is, in a sense, necessary if Herbert's enterprise is
to escape the dangers of an enclosed and purely personal piety
that we have seen threaten the programme for sacred poetry in
its late Renaissance context. 'Providence' has its finely sweeping
moments [e.g. 11 29–32 or 41–4] and it is never less than elegant.
It is only when we compare it with the Old Testament nature
poetry it sometimes evokes, like Psalm 104, that we register how
confining its order is.

Interestingly Herbert is more successful in capturing the
cosmic resonance of his Scripture sources in poems of the
inner life like the two 'Temper' pieces and 'The Flower'.
Behind the latter lie such biblical apprehensions of God as
those of Hannah's prayer: 'The Lord killeth, and maketh alive;
he bringeth down to the grave, and bringeth up' [I Samuel
2:7] but in Herbert their stark juxtapositions have become a
sinuous process and so more disorientating – an effect which
the miniaturising, far from diminishing, intensifies: 'these are
thy wonders, Lord of power,/ Killing and quickning, bringing
down to hell/ And up to heaven in an houre'. Disorientation is
at work differently in 'Mortification', whose boxed-in moralising
can resonate with a haunting irony ('When boyes go first to bed,/

They step into their voluntarie graves . . . Successive nights, like rolling waves,/ Convey them quickly, who are bound for death'). Perhaps most potent of all is the exquisitely piercing turn in 'Discipline':

> Love is swift of foot;
> Love's a man of warre,
>   And can shoot,
> And can hit from farre.
>
> Who can scape his bow?
> That which wrought on thee,
>   Brought thee low,
> Needs must work on me.

The Old Testament God of battles (compare the war-song of Exodus 15: 'The LORD is a man of war: the LORD is his name') and the mischievous Cupid of the love poets are conflated in the image of a divine power which is irresistible because it is the power of a self-sacrificing, self-wounding love.

Herbert: the homely into the strange

Herbert's miniaturising can disorientate where (say) Donne's often achieves effects of a comprehensiveness at once explosive and complete. Disorientation can be achieved by other routes as well, not least when the poetry seems at its most emphatic in the pursuit of the homely or the simple. Sometimes the effect can be lodged in a single word as with the enigmatic verb in 'H. Scriptures' II 'dispersed herbs do watch a potion' or the displaced adjective in 'a ragged noise and mirth' which puckers the deliberately colourless retelling of the Christian story in 'Redemption' and may prepare us for the detonating matter-of-factness of its final line: 'Who straight, *Your suit is granted*, said, & died'.

Disorientation can also be built up through an entire poem as it is in 'The Bag' or 'The Agonie'. The former centres on the piercing of Jesus' side on the cross. It bypasses the traditional interpretation (going back to the Fourth Gospel – see John 19:34–7; and cf. ll 245–7 of *The Sacrifice*) which sees in this episode a prefiguring of the sacraments which take their power from Christ's death. Instead the Incarnation is dovetailed into a nursery–rhyming version of

Old Testament nature poetry [11 8–18; cf. e.g.Psalm 104:1–4]; the actual death of Christ gets a single, almost throwaway line; and the side-piercing is elaborated with a word-play that is both poignant and dry. It is as if the familiar story of Incarnation and Passion were being played out behind rippled glass. The effect is powerfully to *defamiliarise*. The humility of the God who makes himself the servant of his creatures regains its strangeness.

Behind such effects – a long way behind them – lie such opaque gospel sayings as Jesus' proclamation: 'my flesh is meat indeed, and my blood is drink indeed. He that eateth my flesh, and drinketh my blood, dwelleth in me and I in him' [John 6:55–6]. A long way behind them because *part* of what Herbert is doing is to expand such pregnant fusions of the physical and spiritual. In expanding them, in articulating them through effects of fairy tale and pun, he removes that original opacity but makes the connections between the elements he has articulated curiously elusive. We seem to glimpse a world where physical and spiritual are fully, even intensely, integrated but we cannot *quite* tell how and we glimpse it only by standing at an odd angle to the world of our ordinary experience.

Something similar is done – but with a more triumphant effect of defamiliarising – in the closing lines of 'The Agonie': 'Love is that liquor sweet and most divine,/ Which my God feels as bloud; but I, as wine'. The effect here radiates out from keeping the different items – God and man, the love which unites them, the physical blood of Christ, the physical communion wine – sharply separate and no less tautly connected across that separation. Such connection-in-separation is what the metaphysical conceit with its yoking of the heterogeneous is naturally adapted for. Here it works to evoke a mystery (I use the term in the sense sometimes given to it in the philosophy of religion where a *problem* to be *solved* is distinguished from a *mystery* which is to be *contemplated* and which can draw us into itself).

The evoking of mystery – here done through a defamiliarising use of the homely – is one of Herbert's strongest answers to the dangers of the overdomesticated and overcontrolled which threaten him as a religious poet. He can also work towards it in more straightforward ways as in 'Prayer' (I) with its heaping up of definitions richly opaque ('The milkie way, the bird of paradise,/ Church-bels beyond the starres heard, the soules bloud,/ The land of spices') only to cap them with a final definition opaque because transparent: 'something understood'. I have said that transposition is one of the fundamental patterns of Herbert's imagination. Prayer as he conceives it is the most intimate form of the transposition between God and man. The final definition of it in this poem, fusing agnosticism (*something* understood – we cannot specify what) with certainty (something *understood*) might be taken as summing up his achievement as a religious poet. It is an achievement we might salute in lines from a very different master, the American poet Wallace Stevens:

> He is the transparence of the place
> In which he is, and in his poems we find peace.

Vaughan

Vaughan is a disciple of Herbert and a poet of the Interregnum, the name commonly given to the period between the execution (1649) of Charles I and the restoration of his son in 1660; and the second of these facts decisively modifies the first. The preface to the second edition of *Silex Scintillans* in 1655 repeats (in shriller tones) the call of Herbert and others for a purged and exclusive sacred poetry and Herbert is a pervasive presence in the poems that follow. But the distance between him and Vaughan can be measured by their respective poems on 'The British Church'. Herbert's – which has a good claim to be his worst poem – is a classic utterance of Anglican complacency ('Blessed be the God, whose love it was/ To double-moat thee with his grace,/ And none but thee'); Vaughan's is the elegaic cry of the poet of an underground church ('Ah! he is fled!/ And while these here their *mists* and *shadows* hatch/ My glorious head/ Doth on those hills of myrrh, and incense watch'). Other pieces (e.g. the Latin poem 'To Posterity' that prefaces his second collection *Olor Iscanus* and his prose treatises of the early 1650s) make explicit how acutely he experienced the Anglican and royalist defeat in the Civil War.

That experience in turn may be bound up with the religious crisis or conversion of which Vaughan speaks in the Latin poem that prefaces the first edition of *Silex Scintillans*. Most older accounts saw the religious poetry of the latter as breaking radically in style and topic with Vaughan's secular verse and related this break to his conversion. This has been questioned

[Kermode, 1950] and certainly one cannot treat the biography and the poetry as cause and effect, especially when the biography is as sketchy as Vaughan's. Some recent accounts have attended in detail to his second secular collection *Olor Iscanus* (completed in 1647 but not published till 1651 and then perhaps against Vaughan's will) and I would see the true break in his poetry as occurring between this volume and its predecessor, the *Poems* of 1646.

The latter, except for its Juvenal translation, is pastiche, accomplished and empty. *Olor Iscanus* continues both the pastiche and the translation, with poems that recall Jonson or the Donne of the Satires and versions from the Latin of Ovid, Boethius and the Polish Jesuit Casimir. But it can also be read as shaping a carefully composed royalist response to the events of the Civil War. This can be traced in its choice of poems to translate, with the strong emphasis on a poetry of exile and of adversity stoically endured. It can be traced in the handling of such recognised topics as the invitation to a friend and in the powerful Latin poems of pastoral solitude that conclude the volume. On all these counts there are continuities with *Silex Scintillans* and at moments *Olor Iscanus* glimmers with stylistic anticipations of the later Vaughan (see e.g. the opening poem to the River Isca or ll 33–8 of the complimentary poem on Cartwright's works).

But in *Silex Scintillans* (first edition 1650; second, with Part II added, 1655) the motifs and preoccupations of the previous volume have been decisively transformed. The poetry of retreat from the public world has deepened into a poetry of buried life and resurrection. The solitude of pastoral has yielded to a poetry of night and of spiritual exile but exile sometimes vibrant with yearning and with a sense of nature as mysteriously alive or charged with the presence of the divine: 'each *bush*/ And *oak* doth know *I AM*' ('Rules and Lessons'). And, counterpoising these, there is a radiant, intermittent, poetry of renewal. The volume opens with 'Regeneration' which charts a transforming of psychic life and perception:

>   A new spring
>   Did all my senses greet;
>
>   The unthrift Sun shot vital gold
>   A thousand pieces,
>   And heaven its azure did unfold

> Chequered with snowy fleeces,
> The air was all in spice
> And every bush
> A garland wore; thus fed my eyes
> But all the ear lay hush.

This is matched in 'Ascension-Day' which opens Part II:

> I walk the fields of *Bethany* which shine
> All now as fresh as *Eden* and as fine.
> Such was the bright world, on the first seventh day,
> Before man brought forth sin, and sin decay;
> Where like a virgin clad in *flowers* and *green*
> The pure earth sat, and the fair woods had seen
> No frost but flourished in that youthful vest
> With which their great Creator had them dressed:
> When Heaven above them shined like molten glass,
> While springs, like dissolved pearls their streams did pour
> Ne'er marred with floods, nor angered with a shower.

The transformation in the second poem is cosmic, the subject matter biblical and the style burnished and metallic. It is a public poem where 'Regeneration' is a personal one, its style suggestive and sometimes gleamingly opaque. In all these respects the two poems signal the sizeable shift that occurs between the two parts of *Silex Scintillans* but both could fairly be called visionary.

Visionary is a term that may be found irritatingly vague. It involves, at least, the notion of a heightened perception in which persons or scenes and objects in nature are transfigured, seen as radiant, bearers of a revelation that is religious in its gravity and authority. Such a quality is one feature that separates Vaughan's religious poetry decisively from that of his master Herbert. It is also one reason why *Silex Scintillans* is so uneven. No poetry can sustain itself on visionary perceptions throughout: the fundamental problem for all visionary poets is to find structures and a style that will house and integrate the perceptions on which their poetry centres. It is a problem faced by later and greater visionary poets like Wordsworth, Blake and Eliot – all of whom solve it more successfully than Vaughan. Too often in Vaughan a poetry of visionary perception degenerates into dogged moralising or a polemic that is either querulous or shrill. Or the liquid movement of his verse at its best lapses into the rocking-horse rhythms of a bad hymn. Such failures could be put down to simple incapacity were it not that Vaughan in his secular verse had shown himself so smoothly accomplished.

I would suggest two reasons for those failures. One is that neither the model of an ordered cosmos nor the forms of dramatic and didactic lyric Vaughan inherited from Herbert can carry the visionary perceptions crucial to his poetry in *Silex Scintillans*. He can use the old model of the cosmos with its microcosm/macrocosm analogies (as in 'Misery' or 'The Timber') to read off didactic meanings from the natural world. At its best this yields a lucid moralising poetry as in 'The Water-fall'; but compared with the evocation of a charged and integrated universe in a visionary poem like 'Cock-Crowing' one cannot but feel it as limited. To use my earlier formulation, one might say that Vaughan can develop *styles* in which his visionary perceptions can be housed but lacks a *conceptual framework*, a world-view, that can integrate them.

This can, of course, be disputed. Some Vaughan scholars would claim that the Hermetic philosophy on which he draws in 'Cock-Crowing' gives him just such a framework. My own view would be that in his poetry he only employs it intermittently; that it helps create the sense of a universe integrated and mysteriously vibrant which some of the entirely successful poems ('Midnight', 'Cock-Crowing') give; but that it does not act as an ordering frame in the way that Eliot's Anglo-Catholic Christianity does for him in, say, *Little Gidding*. (Contrast, however, Smith [1985].)

The second reason I would suggest is that the unevenness of *Silex Scintillans* can be related to the strains of Vaughan's position as an Interregnum poet. As much as Marvell, he is a poet of the Civil War and its sequels, including the execution of the king and the displacement of the Anglican church which the lines quoted at the start of this section lament. And if the shocks and displacement of the Interregnum helped precipitate a new kind of religious poetry very different from Herbert's they may also have exacted their price. It is Vaughan's relations with Herbert and with his Interregnum context I now want to trace in more detail.

Vaughan and Herbert

Older accounts defined their relation by saying that Vaughan is weak where Herbert is strong – in the control of structure and tone – but with moments of a visionary splendour unknown to Herbert. This is fair enough as far as it goes but it does less than justice to Vaughan's stylistic mastery at his best, his limpid control of syntax and movement and diction. It also fails to capture the variety of relations that exist between different Vaughan and Herbert poems.

As might be expected from the fissure between their historical contexts those relations are least fruitful when most direct. This is clear in the numerous pieces that are tagged or riddled with echoes of the earlier poet – tagged or riddled because the echoes, even if pervasive, remain unassimilated to the texture of Vaughan's own verse. He does better in poems that imitate a Herbert model but generate from their imitation a grave movement of unrest (as in 'Man') or a sweeping drive, both visionary and satirical (as in 'The World'). Better still are those cast or seeded from a Herbert original. By 'cast', I mean poems like 'Holy Scriptures' or 'Son-days' which keep the form and structure of the Herbert but develop it in ways that are distinctively Vaughan: compare the thrust of his 'Holy Scriptures' ('Thou art life's charter, the Dove's spotless nest/ Where souls are hatched unto Eternity') with Herbert's sedater 'Thou art all health, health thriving till it make/ A full eternity' ('H.Scriptures'1). By 'seeded', I mean poems that develop something only hinted at or latent in their originals. Such are 'I walked the other day' in relation to 'The Flower' or the poems of redirected quest like 'Regeneration' or 'The Search' in relation to Herbert's 'Pilgrimage'. The latter is a lucid allegory of toil and frustration. 'Regeneration' keeps that lucidity of allegory but combines it with a laminated imagery, a delicately shifting rhythm, that infuse its quest with a sense of mystery not found in Herbert.

Silex Scintillans can absorb Herbert creatively in all these ways. Nonetheless its imaginative world is very different from that of *The Temple*. Vaughan's focal images are of the seed growing secretly, sparks under ash, a clouded star, sleep as a shroud, the dream or fairy-tale landscape of 'dark hills, swift streams and steep ways/ As smooth as glass' ('Joy of my life'). Stones in Herbert are built into complex images of temple, church monuments and altar. Stones in Vaughan are isolated in a landscape, covenant memorials, charged with an Old Testament mystery or challenge ('The Bird', 'The Stone', 'Jacob's Pillar and Pillow'). *Silex Scintillans* is saturated in biblical allusion but where Herbert's poetry draws primarily on the central story of redemption that arches from the Exodus to Easter, Vaughan's is most richly fed by the patriarchal narratives of Genesis from which he gleans a distinctive pastoral poetry (e.g. 'The Search' or 'Isaac's Marriage'), by the Song of Solomon (which yields him a poetry of yearning rather than the heaped raptures it yields Crashaw), by the eighth chapter of Romans with its hope of a redeemed creation and by the first three chapters of Revelation with their imagery of the white stone, the hidden manna, the morning star.

Vaughan and the Interregnum

A period of acute upheaval and institutional breakdown, such as the early years of the Interregnum, is likely to urge religious sensibility in directions that seem opposed and yet may interact. On the one hand it may lead to a stress on the divine or the sacred as present everywhere in nature and in man ('Everything that lives is holy'); on the other to an acute sense of the present order of things as transient ('Here we have no continuing city') or flawed beyond redemption. In the latter case the divine or the sacred are set radically over against nature and man. Salvation is elsewhere. It may be located in a lost paradise for which we yearn, or in a flight from the present order, or in an apocalyptic deliverance in which that order is overthrown and replaced by one radically new. All these responses flourish in the teeming religious literature of the Interregnum. Sometimes they are freakishly or exuberantly crossed, as they are more than a century later in Blake whom some modern scholars have placed in a subterranean religious tradition that reaches back to the Interregnum sects. *Silex Scintillans* is touched or permeated by all of them and one of Vaughan's tasks as a religious poet is to evolve styles through which they can be expressed and to find ways of integrating the different responses themselves.

Integration is the more difficult for him because the kind of situation sketched above awakens in an acute form the age-long tension within Christianity between attitudes of world-rejection and world-acceptance, between seeing the world as, fundamentally, the good creation of God and now redeemed, and seeing it as fundamentally fallen and to be escaped from, with redemption breaking in, catastrophically, at the end of history.

Styles and responses

The apocalyptic response which looks to the cataclysmic over-throw of the present order is the one Vaughan manages with least success. The poems which handle or approach it (they are more numerous in Part Two) are almost uniformly flat – and the one thing an apocalyptic poetry cannot afford to be is *flat*. He evokes integration and renewal far more successfully through the opposite response – the looking to a pristine, paradisal world. This can be done in a style characterised by a clear chiming music as it is in 'The 'Morning-Watch':

> In what rings,
> And *hymning circulations* the quick world
> Awakes and sings;
> The rising winds,
> And falling springs,
> Birds, beasts, all things
> Adore him in their kinds.
> Thus all is hurled
> In sacred *hymns*, and *order*, the great *chime*
> And *symphony* of nature.

Other poems in this style, like 'Christ's Nativity' and the 'Ascension-Hymn' make its implications clearer. In them the distinctive thin music articulates the yearning to escape from a present life felt as clogging and fleshly. But such a yearning need not be escapist in a perjorative sense. 'Ascension–Day' evokes not a lost Eden but an Eden restored and in the steadily tightening octosyllabic couplets of 'The Retreat' yearning takes on a dance-beat energy: 'Some men a forward motion love,/ But I by backward steps would move,/ And when this dust falls to the urn/ In that state I came return'.

This drives towards a final integration of opposites. Such an integration can also be achieved through a sudden imaginative coup like that which springs magnificently out of the measured movement of 'The Evening-Watch': 'Heaven/ Is a plain watch and without figures winds/ All ages up'. Or it can be pursued more extendedly as it is in Vaughan's poetry of the resurrection whether in the prolonged drifting stanzas of 'Resurrection and Immortality' or in the swifter cyclic movement of the elegies that thread *Silex Scintillans*. (It is this cyclic movement, with its emphasis on waiting and on a buried life, that makes Vaughan's poetry of resurrection so different from the explosive drama of Donne's, even gives him a kinship with a nineteenth-century Christian Romantic writer like George Macdonald.)

The poetry of night and solitude, of death and the buried life can be seen as the negative pole to Vaughan's poetry of the paradisal vision and no less central to his imagination. Its characteristic style is one we might impressionistically describe as 'liquid', a style seen at its finest in 'The Night': 'God's silent searching flight:/ When my Lord's head is filled with dew, and all/ His locks are wet with the clear drops of night'. But 'The Night' also has that vibrancy Vaughan can command ('And what can never more be done,/ Did at midnight speak with the Sun!'). It creates more richly than any other poem in *Silex Scintillans* the sense of God's presence in nature as at once intimate and mysterious. In so doing it takes to its furthest point the first of the responses I mentioned at the beginning of the previous section. That is what makes the more disappointing its lapse in the last two stanzas into a flat world-rejection and a yearning to escape ('O for that night where I in him/ Might live invisible and dim') that seems limp in comparison with the energy and sense of mystery evoked earlier. It is perhaps Vaughan's most characteristic poem both in what it achieves and also in failing to sustain that achievement.

As a coda to it one might take 'I walked the other day'. This has the conversational opening familiar in many Metaphysical poems; its image of the flower recalls Herbert's poem of that name but seems to use it for an allegory more straightforward than anything in the latter. Yet the playing of varied line-length against rhyme pattern generates an almost imperceptible unrest, a refusal to let us settle down into pattern, that prepares us for the sudden mounting and widening movement of the last three stanzas. These deploy effortlessly the weighted and controlling syntax of liturgical prayer. They take the form of a collect: the naked address to the deity ('O thou'), followed by the prolonged adjectival phrase in apposition that evokes the nature or past actions of the God so addressed ('whose spirit did at first inflame etc.') and finally the compacted energy of the verbs that appeal on the basis of that evocation: 'Show me thy peace,/ Thy mercy, love, and ease'. It is less a poem of world-rejection than one which seeks to climb beyond a present world experienced as shadowy in

relation to the transcendent world to which he aspires. But in that
act of climbing the two worlds are found to interpenetrate:

> That in these masques and shadows I may see
> > Thy sacred way,
> And by those hid ascents climb to that day
> > Which breaks from thee
> Who art in all things, though invisibly

and at the very climax when we seem to have left behind 'this
care, where dreams and sorrows reign' we curve poignantly back
to the blank present experience of silence and loss from which (it
is now disclosed) the whole poem began:

> There hid in thee, show me his life again
> > At whose dumb urn
> Thus all the year I mourn.

All these belong to the visionary poetry which, in its differing
styles, is at the centre of Vaughan's work. But the poem with
which I want to end is not visionary in any strong sense, if at all.
It is didactic, expository. It is inspired by Herbert poems like 'The
Quidditie' and 'Prayer' (I) and like them it is a definition poem
whose burden is the falling short inevitable in all definitions. If it
rejects a 'false life' the rejection is given authority by a phrasing
at once brusque and precise:

> > Thou art a moon-like toil; a blind
> > > Self-posing state;
> > A dark contest of waves and wind;
> > A mere tempestuous debate.

This is set against the positive of:

> > Life is a fixed discerning light,
> > > A knowing joy;
> > No chance or fit: but ever bright,
> > And calm and full, yet doth not cloy

with its longer vowel sounds and more spaced-out rhythm which
is also capable (in the last two lines) of a quietly triumphant swing.

Like 'Prayer' (I) it climaxes in a definition at once comprehensive and blank. But where Herbert's 'something understood' is comprehensive by being deliberately indefinite and modest, Vaughan achieves comprehension with a phrase that is evocative, elusive, biblical (with echoes from the story of Genesis chapter 2 where God breathes into the nostrils of man and man becomes a living soul and from the Song of Solomon which is a recurrent homing ground for him throughout *Silex Scintillans*): '*A quickness, which my God hath kissed*'.

Crashaw

Epigram and hymn constitute the twin poles of Crashaw's work. His first volume was a collection of Latin epigrams on Scripture texts. His mature poetry centres in a constellation of hymns: six translated from medieval Latin; the 'Hymn to Saint Teresa' and its two companion pieces; the contrasting Nativity and Epiphany hymns and a few others less notable; with the 'Prayer Book Ode' that is close to the hymns in style. The inherent possibilities of the two forms, at least as Crashaw practises them, seem antithetical. They require or generate opposed styles: the epigram flaunting a witty concentration, the hymn accumulative or orchestrated. Yet much of his poetry, original or translated, modulates between the two.

Crashaw translated (and expanded) several of his own Latin epigrams for his first volume of religious verse in English, the 1646 *Steps to the Temple*. The originals, written in a widespread Renaissance tradition, are unfailingly accomplished. A close translation of that on Matthew 22 reads:

> O Christ, you escape the evil treachery, the Pharisaical nets: and you shatter the pitiful traps with your holy word. Therefore at last they are quiet and keep an unaccustomed silence: in no other way could they speak your [praise] so well.

The English version opens:

> Midst all the darke and knotty Snares
> Black wit or malice can or dares,
> Thy glorious wisdom breaks the Nets
> And treads with uncontrouled steps.

What strikes one here is not just the extending of the Latin but the reined-in power of rhythm this generates, a power culminating in the (very baroque) combination of the pulsing and the statuesque

> Stony amazement makes them stand
> Waiting on thy victorious hand,
> Like statues fixed to the fame
> Of thy renoune, and their owne shame

a combination which is finally locked into oxymoron: 'As if they onely meant to breath,/ To be the Life of their owne death'.

That last line might be called an oxymoron distended half-way to paradox. In paradox contradictory statements are knotted together in such a way that the complete statement seems absurd or self-cancelling. So, a fundamental Christian paradox declares that he who saves his life shall lose it and he who loses his life shall save it. So, in the classic logical paradox of the 'Cretan liar' a Cretan asserts that all Cretans are liars: is the statement true or false? So, one of Donne's impish youthful paradoxes claims that 'Only cowards dare die'. In all these cases paradox works to challenge. Its characteristic effect is at once to baffle and stimulate understanding. It drives us to ask in what sense the self-cancelling statement may be true and in so doing it may draw attention to a deep-seated problem or a deep-seated truth.

In oxymoron the contradictions are more sharply verbal, often, not always, juxtaposing a contradictory adjective and noun. (Shakespeare's Romeo declaims on love as: 'Feather of lead, bright smoke, cold fire, sick health/ Still-waking sleep that is not what it is!' Oxymoron here is extravagant, comic, but it also belongs to the central imaginative pattern of *Romeo and Juliet* and to the fact that it is a tragedy – a very literary tragedy – of love. For oxymoron is a traditional figure in some kinds of love poetry, notably in the Petrarchan tradition whose semi-fossilised conventions Shakespeare in this play can both draw upon and send up.)

Oxymoron is central to Crashaw's work. It is one mark of his kinship with the secular love poets and other features of his poetry group themselves around it: the patterned imagery of mouths–wounds, tears–pearls, blood–roses–rubies; the tensions to be found in his translations of the medieval hymns between the static and the dynamic, between the heightened and the distanced.

Unlike the paradoxes of love in Donne or the paradoxes of Incarnation in Herbert the effects of oxymoron in Crashaw are less analytic than hypnotic. Their danger is that with repetition they will come to seem *only* verbal, a playing with counters, the largeness of the counters – Life, Death, Love – going to intensify the sense of a play that is merely verbal and at the same time high-pitched and exhausting.

This points us towards the deeper limitations of Crashaw as a poet of celebration and of what we may call the religious erotic. (Not that the two are separate: a fusion of the religious and the erotic vibrates through much of his poetry of celebration.)

What I mean by a poetry of celebration is, in the first instance, a poetry that seeks to praise or glorify its subject, a poetry whose key responses are delight or adoration or both. Even when abrupt or vehement in style it is likely to have a strong element of formal patterning as in Smart's *Song to David*, arguably the greatest celebratory poem of the eighteenth century. Such patterning may invoke the ritual and the ceremonial, as in much of Yeats's poetry of celebration. And that, in turn, is related to the fact that a poetry of celebration is inherently *public* to some degree. Spenser's *Epithalamium*, one of the supreme instances of such poetry in English, celebrates a private event – Spenser's own marriage – but it makes of it a public, a ritual, and finally a cosmic, occasion.

Crashaw's poetry is intensely celebratory. It is what most singles him out among the Metaphysicals; it should be part of his value for modern readers who are liable to overvalue a religious poetry of conflict and doubt; and it unquestionably makes him exhilarating to read – for a time. For a time, because if he exhilarates he can also exhaust. Partly this is because the poetry is too unfailingly triumphal. 'Man is a noble animal, splendid in ashes and pompous in the grave, solemnizing nativities and deaths with equal lustre, nor omitting ceremonies of bravery in the infamy of his nature'. What resonates in that famous sentence from Crashaw's contemporary Sir Thomas Browne is a sense of the negative elements in human experience and in the nature of the world that oppose and challenge celebration even if celebration may finally encompass or transcend them. This sense of the negative is strong in some of the greatest cele-bratory artists, in the Chaucer of *Troilus and Criseyde*, for instance, or the Shakespeare of the comedies and the late romances. It is what all celebration that is not to risk lapsing into the facile and exhausting needs to evoke; and it is what Crashaw never gives. Even when he celebrates martyrdom – as he often does – his oxymoronic imagination sucks up suffering, without delay and without remainder, into rapture.

Here as elsewhere our reservations may be with the baroque style at large rather than with Crashaw individually. (One might, though, suggest that his work intensifies the elements modern readers may find problematic in that style. Much baroque art is public, an art of ceremonial and spectacle. Crashaw's, though impersonal, has an enclosed or isolated quality: at worst a hothouse extravagance, at its finest, sometimes, a cloistered opulence.)

Our reservations may be sharpest with his distinctive fusion of the religious and the erotic. I say distinctive because such a fusion is not peculiar to Crashaw. The interconnections of the religious and the erotic or the sexual go deep and have taken widely varied forms, as witness a range of classic texts from Plato's *Symposium* to the poetry of Dante and his fellows to *Wuthering Heights* and *The Rainbow*. Within the Christian tradition the reading of the Song of Solomon as an allegory of the love of Christ for the Church or for the individual soul has provided a rich matrix for exploring the relations of divine and human love. But in all of the texts cited there is movement and development. They do not only celebrate, they explore. In Plato and Dante this takes place in the context of an intellectual and spiritual ascent by which the original human love is purged to become the love of an absolute Beauty or of God. In *Wuthering Heights* and *The Rainbow*, which deploy no such scheme of ascent, there is an opening of the human into the darkly non-human and transcendent.

In Crashaw there is only rapture seized and prolonged:

> O how oft shalt thou complain
> Of a sweet and subtle PAIN
> Of intolerable JOYES;
> Of a DEATH, in which who dyes
> Loves his death, and dyes again,

> And would for ever so be slain.
> And lives and dyes; and knows not why
> To live, But that he may thus never leave to DY.
>
> [*Hymn to Saint Teresa*]

To say that in Crashaw there is '*only* rapture' seems comically ungrateful in the face of such lines which must rank among the finest erotic poetry of the seventeenth century. But if we set the *Hymn* against the poetry of the sixteenth-century Spanish mystic, John of the Cross (friend and collaborator of Saint Teresa) we register Crashaw's limitations. Poems like 'Upon a gloomy night', 'Songs between the soul and the Bridegroom' and 'O flame of love so living' are as intense as anything in Crashaw. But they have a flexibility, a range of tone, that he lacks and because of this their intensity can be felt as *piercing* in a way that Crashaw's never is. (And in saying this one is talking only of the immediate impact of the poems on a reader who knows nothing of Saint John's elaborate exposition of, for instance, 'Upon a gloomy night' as an account of the mystical ascent, by way of negation, to God.)

Again, the two episodes from Teresa's autobiography on which Crashaw builds his hymn – her setting out as a child to convert the Moors and her vision of the angel who pierced her heart with a burning golden dart – are handled by her with a briskness quite lost when she becomes, in the poem, an icon of baroque devotion. (For a much fuller response to Teresa readers should go to Jack Clemo's splendid poem 'Mould of Castile' in which a modern poet of a religious tradition and landscape widely different from Teresa's salutes her as a spirit at once removed and akin.)

That said, it is worth stressing how far Crashaw can extend those limitations, even if he does not finally transcend them. He can do so by his handling of rhythm and tempo. Contrast the weighted and stretching octosyllabic couplets in the opening of the Teresa hymn with its climactic lines quoted earlier and both with the antiphonal climax of 'The Flaming Heart'. He can also do so through conceits whose extravagant elegance creates a simultaneous effect of ardour and distancing. This is what happens in the seraphim-as-Cupids passage of the Teresa hymn [II 91–6]. It is an effect we can see him working towards in some of his translations of medieval hymns.

Translation is an important area of Crashaw's work. Like his revisions of his English poems it lets us grasp something of the craftsmanship we are more than liable to lose sight of in the extravagance of his verse. It shows him moving in opposite directions that can be correlated with the basic oppositions noted at the beginning as characterising his work. There is a movement to elaborate which adds to the original a distinctive sensuousness, whether luscious (as in his paraphrase of Psalm 23) or spongy (as in his translation of the praise of Spring from Virgil's *Georgics*) or merely flabby (as in his woeful attempt on that austerest of Day of Judgement poems, the 'Dies Irae'). Conversely, he can tighten and sharpen his original as he does with Marino's *Sospetto d'Herode* [Praz, 1958, pp.232–8]. As with some other verbally lavish poets – Marlowe and Shelley come to mind – translation may offer a creative resistance to his natural temperament.

The interaction of translator and original can be seen at its most successful in his version of the medieval Passion hymn 'Stabat Mater'. The original appeals directly to the emotions with its short plangent lines, its insistent rhyming, the involvement of its speaker with the suffering Mother and her Son. Around this Crashaw weaves a poetry of elaborated conceits. The final stanza of the Latin has a raw ardour: 'Fac me plagis vulnerari/ Cruce fac inebriari/ et cruore filii' ('Make me to be wounded with [your] blows/ Make me drunk with the cross/ And with the blood of [your] son'). In English it achieves a different kind of intensity, stretching and elegant:

> O let me suck the wine
> So long of this chaste vine
> Till drunk of the dear wounds, I be
> A lost Thing to the world, as it to me.

Translation here may overlap with Crashaw's fusion of secular poetic styles into his religious celebration. There is a long tradition in Christian devotion of the imagery of divine inebriation, a tradition that reaches back to texts like Song of Solomon 2:4–6. In this piece, as in his paraphrase of Psalm 23 or at the end of 'An Apologie for the fore-going Hymne', Crashaw may be drawing on the idiom of Anacreontic drinking song. His friend Cowley in his versions of Anacreon (mentioned at the beginning of Part One) charges the clear-edged music of the Greek originals with a hyperbolical energy. If Crashaw knew these (they were not published till some years after his death so this can only be speculation) he may have found in them a style he could use. Elsewhere his religious poetry of rapture can transpire with the idiom of Carew's luscious elegy of that title and one of his most masculine pieces, the second version of the 'Letter to the Countess of Denbigh', argues in the style of a persuasion-to-love poem like Marvell's 'Coy Mistress'. But always it is a fusion of secular and religious, not the purging of the former which Herbert aims at; and it is this which gives Crashaw's poetry of celebration its unabashed energies and periodically makes it problematic for some readers. (His own few secular love poems have a kind of wax-and-ivory elegance that is very attractive. They suggest the Cavalier lyrists and, behind them, Jonson. They should not be neglected in favour of *Musicks Duell* which too often functions as the showpiece of Crashaw's secular verse.)

It is in the Nativity and Epiphany hymns that Crashaw can be argued to pass beyond the limitations of the work discussed so far and it is with them that I want to end. In the former the accumulation that can overload his other hymns ('Assumption', maybe even the 'Hymn to the Name of Jesus') is marshalled into a choral counterpointing and the intensities of oxymoron are spaced to achieve a comprehensive chiasmic patterning of light and darkness, eclipse and radiance, blindness and vision, a patterning clinched in the poem's key lines:

> Maintaining 'twixt thy world and ours
> A commerce of contrary powers.

The contrasting Nativity hymn might be claimed as the centre of Crashaw's work. It can draw on the secular conventions of pastoral for its adoration. It can expand oxymoron in a celebration that is high-wrought without ceasing to be tender:

> WELLCOME. Though not to gold or silk.
>   To more than Caesar's birthright is;
> Two sister-seas of virgin-Milk
>   With many a rarely—temper'd kisse
> That breathes at once both MAID and MOTHER,
> Warmes in the one, cooles in the other.

And it can carry the ardour of his conceits into such a wholly satisfying coup as:

> The phaenix builds the Phaenix' nest.
> LOVE'S architecture is his own

– a coup matched by the closing lines in which this very un-Herbertian admirer of Herbert makes over into his own idiom one of Herbert's chief emphases:

> Till burnt at last in fire of Thy fair eyes,
> Our selves become our own best SACRIFICE.

Marvell

> Two mirrors with Infinity to dine;
> Drink him below the table when they please.
>
> [Empson]

The subject of Marvell's one devotional lyric, 'The Coronet', is that recurrent burden of Herbert's in *The Temple*: the egoism that seems to twine inescapably about a poetry which aspires to devote itself to God, the egoism that may be inseparable from the activity of writing itself. Herbert wrestles with it repeatedly and his answers are varied. Marvell drives it to an impasse that may only be broken by violence:

> But thou who only couldst the serpent tame,
> Either his slippery knots at once untie;
> And disentangle all his winding snare;
> Or shatter too with him my curious frame,
> And let these wither, so that he may die,
> Though set with skill and chosen out with care.

But how finely poised the violence is between the sinuous movement of that third line quoted and the trailing regret of the last!

I begin with 'The Coronet' because it is characteristic of Marvell in several ways: in its preoccupation with frames and entanglement, in its condensing a topic extensively handled by an earlier poet or poets in a single treatment and in the combination of smoothness and a certain underlying violence with which that treatment is pursued.

'The Definition of Love' stands in a relation not dissimilar to Donne and to his Cavalier followers. As a definition poem it recalls such pieces as 'A Lecture on the Shadow' or 'A Valediction:forbidding Mourning.' It evokes Donne in its tone which is at once extravagant and casual, in the lordliness of its stance and in the drive of its wit. But it is a Donne poem cut free from any sense of situation or relationship (contrast the poems cited as analogues for it); a Donne poem reduced to silhouette. And, in being so reduced, it acquires a certain abstract power (seen in that sudden magnificent turn its conceit makes possible: 'though Love's whole world on us doth wheel').

Taken together these two poems display Marvell's selectivity: the power to seize and concentrate the key features of a chosen model that makes his own poetry, though small in volume, so comprehensive of previous genres and topics and styles. They display the abstraction which can be the price of such selectivity and which would produce skeleton or dessicated poems were it not for the energy that powers them. And they suggest how the trajectory that energy traces is bounded, on the one side, by the elegant, on the other by the violent.

Such a trajectory is traced by Marvell's greatest poem, the *Horatian Ode*; and a similar energy is at work, if mutedly and sporadically, in that other major meditation in time of civil war, *Upon Appleton House*. But though I have begun with poems that look to Herbert and Donne, and though Marvell responds to a range of other masters and models, not least Horace, his most immediate affinities, it seems to me, are with the Cavalier poets and especially with their most prodigal talent, Lovelace.

The Cavalier poets – at any rate the three connected with the Court, Carew, Suckling and Lovelace (Herrick is a quite different kind of poet) – have been classed as heirs both of Donne and Jonson. One can point, especially in Carew, to specific poems imitated; imitated but, in Carew at least, reduced, made elegant and lightweight. Cavalier love poetry as a whole might be characterised as a poetry of flirtation that can dwindle into the trivial or the coarse-fibred. Marvell proclaims his affinity with it in lyrics of wrought compliment like 'The Fair Singer' or compliment suavely mocking and detached like 'Mourning'. But even in the latter a distinctive note sounds in lines like:

And, while vain pomp does her restrain

> Within her solitary bow'r,
> She courts herself in am'rous rain;
> Herself both Danae and the show'r.

The interest in self-enclosure is characteristic; so also is the curious energy it generates. And the last stanza steps back into the quizzical detachment ('I yet my silent judgment keep/ Disputing not what they believe') that infiltrates so much of Marvell.

Sometimes he reaches that detachment through framing devices as in 'The Gallery'; sometimes through a manic cultivation of the hyperbole inherent in the conceit as with 'The Unfortunate Lover'. Nor is this confined to his consummating of the Cavalier lyric: detachment through framing is at the heart of 'The Garden'. And beyond detachment through framing and hyperbole lies the detachment of Marvell's poetry of self-enclosure – though this too has its Cavalier antecedent in the poetry of Lovelace.

The latter stands out against Carew and Suckling as having a quality of ragged splendour that makes him the most notable of the three. But ragged should be given equal stress with splendour. In some of his lyrics a singing line or image will be tangled in extravagant elaborations (e.g. 'Lucasta's World'); conceits will tumble into the lumpy and grotesque (e.g. 'Love Made in the First Age' which vulgarises both the naturalism of some Renaissance pastoral [11 7–24] and Donne's 'Relic' [11 49–54]). A strain of the brutal runs through his Cavalier suavity. It is indeed the presence of the brutal in the suave that gives one of his most notable lyrics, 'La Bella Bona Roba', its gamey power.

Marvell wrote commendatory verses for Lovelace's poems in roughly energetic couplets that look back to Donne as his later couplet poems on Cromwell point towards the Augustan. He shares with Lovelace a fascination with the small scale and the enclosed. Both of them carry the miniaturising of the Meta-physical style into the miniscule and the self-reflexive [cf. Ricks in Patrides, 1978]. But in Lovelace this poetry of the miniscule is a dead-end or a simple retreat. In Marvell it can be played with in tantalising ways (the Mower poems); it can be strenuously pur-sued to a final release (as in a 'Drop of Dew'); it can be the starting point for an elaborate interplay of engagement and withdrawal (as in *Upon Appleton House*). And where the suave and the brutal jostle uneasily in Lovelace, Marvell can transcend both in the kind of energy I have suggested at the beginning of this section.

One source of that energy comes from the readiness with which he can deploy macrocosm/microcosm analogies. For if he is very much a second-generation poet in his consummating and his miniaturising he also commands a range beyond any other of the second-generation Metaphysicals. This is seen at its most extended and most puzzling in *Upon Appleton House*.

It takes its place within a genre instituted by Jonson's *To Penshurst*: the country house poem, celebrating a particular estate and its family and the virtues claimed as embodied in their way of life. Its opening stretch [sts 1–40] deploys recognised conventions of the genre: celebration of the actual house's lack of ostentation [sts 4–10] and of the family's virtues and past [sts 11–36]. The former, however, is tagged with the extravagances of a second-generation Metaphysical poetry [sts 6-7] and with Marvell's characteristic entwining puns ('whose columns should so high be raised/ To arch the brows that on them gazed'). The latter combines this kind of punning ('the nun's smooth tongue has sucked her in') with a pantomime-style scene-shifting [sts 32–4] that anticipates the more sustained scene-shifting later [e.g.sts 56 and 59].

The second section [sts 41–58] works problems and controversies of contemporary history into a sportive survey of the Nun Appleton estate and its activities. The scale-shifting of micro/macrocosm play can be deployed here with vertiginous effect [st 47]. One result is to make fluid and disorientating what might seem to be offered as rather flat or, at best, journalistically neat, allegory (mowing as an image of war, the Levellers in st 57). This climaxes in the description of the flood which introduces the third section [sts 59–82] where the poet-speaker retreats into the woods.

There the motifs of retreat and solitude are given their most extended play in Marvell, as are his entwining puns [e.g. sts 74 and 81]. The question – to which I have no confident answer – is: how are we to read all this? As only an escapist extravagance? That might seem to be suggested by its elaborated fantasy [sts 71–80] and by the dismissive close [sts 81–2]. Yet I find it difficult to play down the vibrant energy that seems to emerge from the centre of the fantasy: 'But I on it [the world] securely play,/ And gall its horsemen all the day' [st 76]. And the invoking of the young Maria Fairfax as a cosmic ordering principle, to which the final section [sts 82–97] turns, can hardly be read with literal seriousness either. But if not, how is it to be read? As knowingly hyperbolical compliment? That might hold for the allusion to the Last Judgement in st 86 and yet one might hear a deeper resonance in the allusion to the Fall that counterbalances it in st 96 ('Tis not, what once it was, the world,/ But a rude heap together hurled,/ All negligently overthrown') and in the climaxing invocation of Maria herself: 'You, heaven's centre, Nature's lap/ And paradise's only map').

Upon Appleton House is one of the most capacious of Metaphysical poems. It is capacious not in the intense concentrating fashion of the miniaturising Metaphysical lyric but with the flexibility of the 'easy philosopher' (st 71). Its central problem is how we read this figure, whose consciousness might seem to give the poem coherence if anything does. And that returns us to the topics of stance, elusiveness, framing, mirroring and all-but-infinite regress that continue to occupy discussion of Marvell.

Questions of stance in the *Horatian Ode* have also raised much controversy. But its style differs radically from that of *Upon Appleton House*. It is powered by a snaking energy of rhythm that can coil itself in epigram ('Nature, that hateth emptiness/ Allows of penetration less') or expand to encompass Cromwell's rise with an extraordinary evocation of its widening power:

> Who, from his private gardens, where
> He lived reservèd and austere,
>   As if his highest plot
>   To plant the bergamot,
> Could by industrious valour climb
> To ruin the great work of time,
>   And cast the kingdoms old
>   Into another mould.

In one sense it could hardly be called a Metaphysical poem at all but not even the sketchiest account of Marvell could leave it unmentioned. And it does bring into play more urgently than any of his other poems some of his central preoccupations: with the issues of engagement in action versus withdrawal, as these are embodied in the paradigmatic figures of Cromwell and Charles I; and with the use of frames as these work in the three panels of the poem's action. The first [ll 1–52] evokes Cromwell's rise with a strange dream-like clarity, the third [ll 65–120] celebrates him as the master-general of the new Republic and between them is held the perfectly staged drama of Charles's execution. The elegant nobility with which he acts out his doom is rightly celebrated. What we should also note is that *acting* (in the theatrical sense, but with no suggestion of an undercutting sneer) is the only action now open to him. Note also the interaction of this poised drama both with the Machiavellian plotting attributed to Cromwell in the lines that precede and with the violent, exultant energies of revolutionary politics in the lines that immediately follow. ('This was that memorable hour/ Which first assured the forced power'.) But the energies so powerfully evoked undergo a significant change. Cromwell, the supreme man of action, is now seen as enclosed within the historical processes that he has moulded and which there is no suggestion he will not continue triumphantly to control. Only there is a difference between his evocation in the first section as a force of nature in the thunderbolt image, almost as a mythic figure, and the final exhortations to the successful general-politician who must move in a world of specifically plotted campaigns and political manoeuvre: 'But thou, the Wars' and Fortune's son,/ March indefatigably on', reminded that 'the same arts that did gain/ A power, must it maintain'. The energy that drives the poem from its start is still there but the tempo has altered decisively.

In its evocative power and its insight into the nature and ironies of historical process and especially of revolutionary change the *Horatian Ode* can be claimed as the greatest political poem in the language. More than anything else it calls to mind Shakespeare's exploration of power politics and political theatre in his history plays as that runs on into *Hamlet's* meditation on what it means or might mean to play the king. (And consider the drama of the abdication scene in *Richard II* with its twining of passivity and power in the figure of the politically defeated king in relation to the 'tragic scaffold' of Marvell's Charles; or the figure of Bolingbroke, as the *Henry IV* plays develop, in relation to Marvell's Cromwell. I am not suggesting direct parallels, only that they throw cross-lights upon each other.)

And, having intermittently suggested connections in this study between Metaphysical poetry and other areas of Renaissance literature from which it should not be divorced, I am happy to end with this one.

Conclusion

DISCUSSING the American poetess Marianne Moore in his study of *Poetry and Possibility* Michael Edwards remarks that 'while strange similes are easy, truly strange ones are rare, the doors to understanding'. That probing formula focuses the question that, as I claimed in the Introduction, Metaphysical poetry presses on its readers: the question we make preliminary gestures towards defining when we characterise this poetry as bizarre, striking, extravagant, quaint or grotesque.

We can take extravagant as the middle term of that list. Its root meaning is 'wandering beyond [boundaries]'. (The Ghost in *Hamlet* is characterised as, in this sense, an 'extravagant and erring spirit'.) Metaphysical poetry commonly crosses boundaries, disrupts expectations, snatches at attention by its strangeness, most obviously the strangeness of its similes when simile is pushed over into conceit.

As Edwards says, such strangeness is easy and in some Metaphysical poetry it is no more than a trick and the poems only party-trick pieces to be enjoyed, if at all, as such. Cleveland is the stock example here. (My own view would be that he deserves rather better than to function as the textbook figure of Metaphysical decadence. He can combine extravagance of conceit with an engaging lightness of rhythm in a lyrical piece like 'Upon Phillis walking' which Marvell found worth using in *Appleton House*; his all-but-apoplectic satires can put a like extravagance to some use; and I confess to enjoying even such a machine-gun performance as his elegy for Edward King (Milton's Lycidas), though I admit its pleasures are of a kind to be taken in modest doses.)

But Metaphysical extravagance can also fork towards the strange. We have seen how Herbert comes to such strangeness through his cultivation of the homely. The strangeness we encounter in Crashaw may be mostly that of a style (the baroque) that is historically remote from us. In Vaughan it may be partly due to the Hermetic images and concepts that, again, we find remote. But I think his poetry can lodge a strangeness more stubbornly other. Much of it voices experiences that are common enough: restlessness, bereavement, political complaint, the yearning for a lost innocence of childhood or a past golden age. But ever and again there cut into these glimpses of another order of experience altogether. The elegy beginning 'They are all gone into the world of light' sustains the low-keyed lucidity of one kind of good hymn. Its second stanza tinges this lucidity with a suggestion of mystery ('It glows and glitters in my cloudy breast/Like stars upon some gloomy grove'), only for the third to break in abruptly upon this with the full visionary perception:

> I see them walking in an air of glory
> Whose light doth trample on my days

the abruptness focused in that use of 'trample' which is completely unexpected but also, here, completely right.

Perhaps the most potent instances of Metaphysical strangeness come in Donne and Marvell. In the latter's 'Mower to Glowworms' what seems only a playful, ceremonious miniaturising:

> Ye country comets, that portend
> No wars, nor prince's funeral,
> Shining unto no higher end
> Than to presage the grass's fall

passes smoothly at the end into radical disorientation:

> Your courteous lights in vain you waste,
> Since Juliana here is come,
> For she my mind has so displaced
> That I shall never find my home.

In Donne's 'Nocturnal upon S. Lucy's Day' the extravagant comparisons become only a means to articulate a grief they increasingly charge with strangeness as we move from the conceit of the stars as gunpowder flasks in stanza 1 to the image of love as alchemy in stanza 2 with its twinning of abstract nouns and adjectives that give the abstractions a hovering physical life: 'from dull privations, and lean emptiness/He ruined me, and I am re-begot/Of absence, darkness, death; things which are not'. These paradoxes of negation are at the core of the situation 'A Nocturnal' creates and explores. The next two stanzas *use* them to analyse what this central stanza had presented as a mystery and in the final stanza mystery returns as we move from the desolation of its opening line – 'But I am none; noor will my sun renew' – to what can be felt as an extraordinary blending of desolation and bouyancy:

> Since she enjoys her long night's festival,
> Let me prepare towards her, and let me call
> This hour her vigil, and her eve, since this
> Both the year's and the day's deep midnight is.

A blending *felt* but not understood in any analytic or comprehending way. And there we might come back to Edwards's phrase and say the strangeness gives us a *door* to understanding.

'A Nocturnal' displays the strangeness of Metaphysical poetry at its most commanding. But such strangeness (using what are genuinely metaphysical concepts, as Herbert uses biblical images and stories, to evoke a mystery) represents only one extreme of this poetry as the party-trick cleverness of, for example, a Cleveland represents another. 'Air and Angels' can use metaphysical concepts no less strenuously to articulate a love relationship with a radiant elegance whose ambience nonetheless remains entirely mundane: a rapt courtesy modulating at the end into the suave. It points us to the area where much Metaphysical poetry groups itself, between the extremes I have cited; a poetry where extravagance can be disciplined into acrobatic play, a poetry offering at its best, the most civilised and resourceful body of lyric in English.

References

I HAVE divided this into five sections: (1) editions and anthologies; (2) literary histories; (3) general accounts of Metaphysical poetry; (4) studies of context; (5) criticism of the individual Metaphysical poets.

Editions

The Cavalier Poets, ed. T. Clayton (Oxford, 1978).
Metaphysical Lyrics and Poems of the Seventeenth Century, ed. H.J.C. Grierson (Oxford, 1921).
The Metaphysical Poets, ed. H. Gardner (London, 1957; rptd OUP, 1967).
Cowley, *Poems*, ed. A.R. Waller (Cambridge, 1905).
Crashaw, *Poems*, ed. L.C. Martin (Oxford, 1957).
——, *Complete Poetry*, ed. G. Williams (New York, 1972).
Donne, *Complete English Poems*, ed. A.J. Smith (London, 1973).
Herbert, *The English Poems of George Herbert*, ed. C.A. Patrides (London, 1974).
Herbert, *Works*, ed. F.E. Hutchinson (Oxford, 1941).
Marvell, *Complete Poems*, ed. E.S. Donno (London, 1974).
Vaughan, *Complete Poems*, ed. A. Rudrum (London, 1976).

Literary history

Auerbach, E., *Mimesis* (Princeton, 1953).
——, 'Sermo Humilis', in *Literary Language and its Public* (Princeton, 1965), pp.27-66.
Colie, R.L., *The Resources of Kind* (Berkeley, 1973).
Duncan, J.E., 'The Revival of Metaphysical Poetry, 1872–1912', *Proceedings of the Modern Language Association*, LXVIII (1953), 658–71.

Eliot, T.S., 'Milton (II)', in *On Poetry and Poets* (London, 1957), pp.146–61.

——, 'What Dante Means to Me', in *To Criticize the Critic* (London, 1965), pp.125–35.

Gillespie, S.F., *The Poets on the Classics* (London, 1988).

Heaney, S., 'Feeling into Words', in *Preoccupations: Selected Prose 1968–78*, new edn (London, 1984), pp.41–60.

Kermode, F., 'Dissociation of Sensibility' in J.R. Roberts (ed.), *Essential Articles: John Donne's Poetry* (Connecticut, 1975), pp. 66–82.

Leavis, F.R., *Revaluation* (London, 1936).

Rhodes, N., *The Elizabethan Grotesque* (London, 1980).

Ricks, C.B. (ed.), *English Poetry and Prose, 1540–1670* (London, 1970).

Tillotson, K., 'Donne's Poetry in the Nineteenth Century (1800–72)', in Roberts (1975), pp.20–33.

Tomlinson, C., *Poetry and Metamorphosis* (Cambridge, 1983).

Winters, Y., 'Aspects of the Short Poem in the English Renaissance', in *Forms of Discovery* (Chicago, 1967), pp.1–120.

General accounts

Coleridge, S.T., *Biographia Literaria*, Everyman edn (rptd London, 1967).

Coleridge on the Seventeenth Century, ed. R.F. Brinkley (1955; rptd New York, 1968).

Eliot, T.S., 'The Metaphysical Poets', in *Selected Essays*, 3rd edn (London,1951), pp.281-91.

Ellrodt, R., *Les Poètes métaphysiques anglais* (Paris, 1960).

Empson, W., *Seven Types of Ambiguity*, 3rd edn (London 1953).

Grierson, H.J.C., 'The Metaphysical Poets', in *The Background to English Literature* (London, 1925), pp.116–65.

Johnson, S., *Life of Cowley*, in *Lives of the Poets*, ed. Hill (Oxford, 1905); rptd (with omissions) in *Samuel Johnson*, ed. D. Greene (Oxford Authors) (Oxford, 1984), pp.677–87; rptd in *Johnson as Critic*, ed. J. Wain (London, 1973), pp.253–68.

Smith, J., 'On Metaphysical Poetry', in F.R. Leavis (ed.), *A Selection from Scrutiny 2* (Cambridge, 1968), pp.157–71.

Context studies

Colie, R.L., *Paradoxia Epidemica* (Princeton, 1966).
Freeman, R., *English Emblem Books* (London, 1948).
Jones, R.F., *The Triumph of the English Language* (Oxford, 1953).
Lewalski, B., *Protestant Poetics and the Seventeenth Century Religious Lyric* (Princeton, 1979).
Martz, L., *The Poetry of Meditation* (Yale, 1952).
Praz, M., *Studies in Seventeenth Century Imagery*, 2nd edn (Rome, 1964).
Røstvig, M.-S., *The Happy Man*, 2 vols (Oslo, 1954–8).
Scoular, K., *Natural Magic* (Oxford, 1965).
Skrine, P., *The Baroque* (London, 1978).
Smith, A.J., *The Metaphysic of Love* (Cambridge, 1985).
Warnke, F.J., *Versions of Baroque* (Yale, 1972).

Criticism of individual poets

(a) Cowley

Trotter, D., *The Poetry of Abraham Cowley* (London, 1979).

(b) Crashaw

Adams, R.M., 'Taste and Bad Taste in Metaphysical Poetry: Crashaw and Dylan Thomas', rptd in W.R. Keast (ed.), *Seventeenth Century Poetry* (New York, 1962), pp.264-79.
Bertanosco, M., *Crashaw and the Baroque* (Alabahma, 1971).
Cooper, R.M. (ed.) *Essays on Richard Crashaw* (Salzburg, 1979).
Eliot, T.S., 'A Note on Richard Crashaw' in *For Lancelot Andrewes* (London, 1927; rptd 1970), pp.92–8.
Healy, T.F., *Richard Crashaw* (Leiden, 1986).
Praz, M., 'The Flaming Heart: Richard Crashaw and the Baroque', in *The Flaming Heart* (New York, 1958), pp.204–63.
Rickey, M.E., *Rhyme and Meaning in Richard Crashaw* (Lexington, 1961).
Warren, A., *Richard Crashaw* (London, 1939).
Williams, G., *Image and Symbol in the Sacred Poetry of Richard Crashaw* (Columbia, 1963).
Young, R.V., *Richard Crashaw and the Spanish Golden Age* (Yale, 1982).

(c) Donne

Bennet, J., 'The Love Poetry of John Donne', rptd in W.R. Keast (ed.), *Seventeenth Century Poetry* (New York, 1962), pp.111–31.

Carey, J., *John Donne: Life, Mind, Art* (London, 1981).

Crofts, J.E.V., 'John Donne: A Reconsideration', rptd in H. Gardner (ed.), *John Donne (Twentieth Century Views)* (New Jersey, 1962), pp.77–89.

Everett, B., 'Donne: a London Poet', in *Poets in Their Time* (London, 1986), pp.1–31.

Gardner, H., 'The Argument about "The Ecstasy"', rptd in J.R. Roberts (ed.), *Essential Articles: John Donne's Poetry* (Connecticut, 1975), pp.239–58.

Guss, D.L., *John Donne, Petrarchist* (Detroit, 1966).

Leishman, J.B., *The Monarch of Wit*, 6th edn (London, 1962).

Lewis, C.S., 'Donne and Love Poetry in the Sixteenth Century', in *Selected Literary Essays* (Cambridge, 1969). Also in Gardner (1972), pp.90–9 and in Keast (1962), pp.92–110.

Sanders, W., *John Donne's Poetry* (Cambridge, 1971).

Smith, A.J., *Donne: Songs and Sonnets* (London, 1964).

(d) Herbert

Bell, I., '"Setting Foot into Divinity": George Herbert and the English Reformation', in J.R. Roberts (ed.), *Essential Articles: George Herbert* (Connecticut, 1979), pp.63–83.

Bloch, C., *Spelling the Word* (Berkeley, 1985).

Davie, D., Introduction to *The New Oxford Book of Christian Verse* (Oxford, 1981).

Eliot, T.S., Review of *Georgian Poetry* in *Athenaeum* (11 April, 1919).

——, 'Religion and Literature' in *Selected Essays*, 3rd edn (London 1951), pp.388-401.

——, 'What is Minor Poetry?' in *On Poetry and Poets* (London, 1957), pp.39–52.

——, *George Herbert* (London, 1962).

Fish, S.E., *Self-Consuming Artifacts* (Berkeley, 1972).

——, *The Living Temple* (Berkeley, 1978).

Nuttall, A.D., *Overheard by God* (London, 1980).

Rickey, M.E., *Utmost Art (Lexington, 1966)*.

Strier, R., *Love Known* (Chicago, 1983).

Summers, J.H., *George Herbert* (London, 1954).
Tuve, R., *A Reading of George Herbert* (Chicago, 1952; rptd 1982).
Vendler, H., *The Poetry of George Herbert* (Harvard, 1975).

(e) Marvell

Brooks, C., 'Marvell's *Horatian Ode*', rptd in M. Wilding (ed.), *Marvell (Modern Judgements)* (London, 1969), pp.93–113.
Bush, D., 'Marvell's *Horatian Ode*', rptd in Wilding (1969), pp.114–24.
Carey, J. (ed.), *Andrew Marvell* (Penguin Critical Anthologies) (London, 1969).
——, 'Reversals transposed: An aspect of Marvell's imagination', in C.A. Patrides (ed.), *Approaches to Marvell* (London, 1978), pp.136–54.
Colie, R.L., *'My Echoing Song'* (Princeton, 1970).
Eliot, T.S., 'Andrew Marvell', in *Selected Essays*, 3rd edn (London, 1952), pp.292–304, rptd in M. Wilding (ed.), *Marvell* (London, 1969), pp.45–66.
Everett, B., 'Poetry and Politics in Andrew Marvell' in *Poets in Their Time* (London, 1986), pp.32–71.
Friedman, D.M., *Marvell's Pastoral Art* (London, 1970).
Kermode, F., 'The Argument of Marvell's *The Garden*', rptd in Wilding (1969), pp.125-40.
Leishman, J.B., *The Art of Marvell's Poetry*, 2nd edn (London, 1968).
Ricks, C.B., '"Its own resemblance"', in Patrides (1978), pp.108–35.
Smith, A.J., 'Marvell's Metaphysical Wit', in Patrides (1978), pp.56–86.
Wallace, J.M., *Destiny his Choice* (Cambridge, 1968).
Wilcher, R., *Andrew Marvell* (Cambridge, 1985).

(f) Vaughan

Bird, M., 'Nowhere but in the dark: On the poetry of Henry Vaughan', in A. Rudrum (ed.), *Essential Articles:Henry Vaughan* (Connecticut, 1987), pp.278–97.
Calhoun, T.O., *Henry Vaughan* (Newark, 1980).

Hill, C., 'Henry Vaughan', in *Collected Essays*, vol.1 (Brighton, 1985), pp.207–15.

Holmes, E., *Henry Vaughan and the Hermetic Philosophy* (Oxford, 1932).

Kermode, F., 'The Private Imagery of Henry Vaughan', *Review of English Studies*, new series 1 (1950), pp.206–25.

Mahood, M.M., 'Vaughan: the Symphony of Nature', in Rudrum (1987), pp.5–45.

Martin, L.C., 'Henry Vaughan and the Theme of Infancy', in Rudrum (1987), pp.46–58.

——, 'Henry Vaughan and "Hermes Trismegistus"', in Rudrum (1987), pp.59–67.

Pettet, E.C., *Of Paradise and Light* (Cambridge, 1960).

Post, J.F.S., *Henry Vaughan* (Princeton, 1982).

Rudrum, A., *Henry Vaughan* (University of Wales, 1981).

Trickett, R., 'Henry Vaughan and the Poetry of Vision', in Rudrum (1987), pp.278–97).

Further
Reading

THOSE who read French should certainly look at Ellrodt, at least on poets they are interested in. On individual Metaphysical poets: Herbert criticism continues to multiply in quantity and elaboration. Some of its developments can be sampled in the collection of essays edited by C.J. Summers and T.–L. Pebworth, *Too Rich to Clothe the Sunne* (Pittsburgh, 1980), where the pieces by M. di Cesare on 'Herbert's *Prayer (I)* and the Gospel of John' and A.C. Fowler on the 'Affliction' poems bear on topics touched on in the Herbert section of this study. The Oxford Authors edition of Herbert and Vaughan by L. Martz not only makes comparison between the two easier but usefully reprints Herbert's prose treatise *A Priest to the Temple*. Those interested in questions of Vaughan's Hermeticism may pursue them further in the articles by A. Rudrum and A.V. Chapman in *Essential Articles: Henry Vaughan*. Discussion of Marvell's politics is elaborated in A.M. Patterson's *Marvell and the Civic Crown* (New Jersey, 1978) and W. Chernaik's *The Poet's Time* (Cambridge, 1983) both of which develop their views to some extent in critical dialogue with Wallace's earlier study. For seventeenth-century political poetry more at large I. Rivers's *Poetry of Conservatism* (Cambridge, 1973) will be found stimulating.

This last item has carried us across into general studies. J. Briggs, *This Stage Play World* (Oxford, 1983) gives an excellent concise account of cultural and social contexts for English literature between 1580 and 1625. G. Parfitt's comprehensive survey *English Poetry of the Seventeenth Century* (London, 1985) combines an approach through genre with a sketching of social and political history. It also supplies a useful chronology and bibliographies. Finally J. H. Summers, *The Heirs of Donne and Jonson* (London, 1970) might be recommended as an engagingly relaxed and civilised piece of literary history.

However good such surveys may be there is no substitute for reading the primary texts. ('First-hand knowledge', C. S. Lewis once wrote, 'is not only more worth acquiring than second-hand knowledge, but is usually much easier and more delightful to acquire'.) With this in mind I append a short list of works relevant to some of the authors and topics discussed.

The ultimate origins of Renaissance Platonic and Neo-Platonic treatments of love are in Plato's *Symposium* (Penguin translation by W. Hamilton). For the Petrarchan tradition S. Minta's anthology *Petrarch and Petrarchism* provides a thorough survey which can be followed up by R.M. Durling's bilingual edition of *Petrarch's Lyric Poetry* (Harvard University Press). Marlowe's translation of Ovid's *Amores* is available in *The Complete Poems and Translations*, ed. Orgel (Penguin). It may be compared with or supplemented by the modern translations of G. Lee, *Ovid's Amores* (John Murray) or P. Green, *Ovid: the Erotic Poems* (Penguin). Horace's *Odes* may be sampled in the older Penguin translation by J. Michie. For the sixteenth-century Spanish mystics there are translations of the *Life of Saint Teresa* by J.M. Cohen (Penguin) and of the *Poems* of John of the Cross by Roy Campbell (Collins). Lastly two anthologies: *Baroque Poetry*, ed. J.P. Hill and E. Caracciolo-Trejo (Everyman) and *English Pastoral Poetry: from the Beginnings to Marvell*, ed. F. Kermode (Harrap) with an introduction that ranges lucidly from Theocritus to John of the Cross.

Index